THE CONSTRUCTIVE PROGRAMMES OF MAHATMA GANDHI

The Constructive Programmes of Mahatma Gandhi

(1920 to 1939)

RADHEY SHYAM SINGH

Commonwealth

The Constructive Programmes of Mahatma Gandhi

ISBN : 81-7169-160-9

Edition : 2026

Published by :
COMMONWEALTH PUBLISHERS (P) LTD.
4831/24, Govind Lane,
Ansari Road, Darya Ganj,
New Delhi - 110002
Ph. : 23272541, 23242541
e-mail : commonwealthpublishers2016@gmail.com

Distributed by :
ARJUN PUBLISHING HOUSE
4831/24, Govind Lane,
Ansari Road, Darya Ganj,
New Delhi - 110002
Ph. : 23272541, 23242541
e-mail : arjunbooks2001@gmail.com

Laser Typesetting by :
Dimple Computers
Delhi

Printed at :
Divine Digital Press
Delhi

Dedication

This book is dedicated to my respected late father, Pavitra Singh and my mother, the late Daulati Devi, who had been the real source of inspiration in my intellectual pursuits.

Acknowledgements

The subject, dealing with a particular aspect of India's freedom movement, has attracted my attention long ago and I have since been working on the subject to arrive at judicious conclusions on the basis of original materials collected through various sources. Some of my revered preceptors have always encouraged me to pursue research work with missionary zeal and I have no hesitation in acknowledging that the present work is essentially an embodiment of their blessings. I am particularly grateful to my guide Dr. Ran Vijoy Kumar, Lecturer in History, Patna College, Patna, who has extended to me all help in preparing this dissertation. I am also thankful to Dr. V.A. Narayan, University Professor and Head of the Department of History, Patna University, Patna for his encouragement and kind suggestions. My thanks are also due to Dr. Birendra Verma, University Professor and Head of the Department of History, Patna College, Patna and Dr. P. Datta, Lecturer in History, Patna University, Patna for lending their valuable services in the writing of this work. I am also grateful to Sri Shankar Dayal Singh, Ex M.P., Secretary, Sri B.N. Pandey, Principal, Sri Nirmal Kumar Srivastava, Vice-Principal of B.D. Evening College, Mithapur, Patna who have extended all affection and blessings to me in this maiden adventure.

I am thankful to the authorities of National Archives. New Delhi, State Archives, Patna, Khuda Bakhsh Library,

Bihar Research Society, District Record Offices, Sadaquat Ashram, Patna, Gandhi Sangrahalaya, Patna, Sinha Library, Patna, A.N. Sinha Institute, Patna, Patna College Library, Patna, National Library, Calcutta and other places for the courtesy and help extended to me during my visit to those institutions.

RADHEY SHYAM SINGH

Abbreviations

A.I.C.C.	=	All India Congress Committee
P.C.C.	=	Provincial Congress Committee
A.I.S.A.	=	All India Spinners' Association
D.I.G.	=	Deputy Inspector General
P.S.	=	Police Station
I.G.	=	Inspector General
S.P.	=	Superintendent of Police
I.P.C.	=	Indian Penal Code
Cr. P.C.	=	Criminal Procedure Code

Contents

Introduction

This research investigation is devoted to present in detail some of the significant aspects of the constructive programmes of Mahatma Gandhi in Bihar and their impact on the socio-economic and political life of the people of this province, who upheld the banner of the national movement with all zeal and enthusiasm. However, to present all these important facets would be an unhill task, for Gandhi sought to bring about radical changes in all walks of the life of the people without breaking away from the cultural traditions of the past. From the year 1920 onwards, Gandhi made numerous such experiments on the basis of his two gospels—truth and non-violence—and it would be interesting to note that these experiments were first tried and successfully tested in this province of Bihar.

The year 1920 has, no doubt, been a landmark in the history of Indian National Movement and it has rightly been regarded as the inauguration of Gandhian era, which ultimately emancipated the country from the yoke of foreign domination. The two significant chapters of India's national struggle—Non-Cooperation Movement and Civil Disobedience Movement—opened up new vistas of constitutional weapons in the hands of the people of Bihar as well as the whole of India and the successes achieved through these weapons aroused feelings of confidence among the people in driving out the alien rulers from the soil of their motherland.

The struggle for freedom under the leadership of Mahatma had negative and positive approaches. Negatively it has in mind boycott of foreign goods and launching civil disobedience against the British imperialist. But positively speaking, the programmes included among other things, development of indigenous production particularly mass production of Khadi and handloom cloths, establishment of national educational institutions, establishment of Panchayats, removal of untouchability, promotion of Hindu-Muslim unity or communal harmony and thereby strengthening the national organisation of the Indian masses, Indian National Congress. In all these programmes, Bihar played a leading role and a number of national leaders including Rajendra Prasad made frequent visits to the different parts of the province and encouraged the people in making the programmes successful from all points of view. Bihar, no doubt, set an example by following the constructive programmes of Gandhi in words and deeds.

Many secondary books on modern history have dwelt at length the various aspects of the Indian national movement. Mention may be made of the works of Ishwari Prasad, Henry Dodwell, S.R. Sharma, D.P. Mukherji, Abdullah Usuf Ali, the series of volumes under the editorship of R C. Mazumdar, the works of B.N. Pandey, Ram Gopal and D. Singh, K.M. Pannikar, R.P. Dutt, K.K. Dutta, Tara Chand and M.N. Das. These works deal in general with the different aspects of Indian National Movement but in none of the books emphasis has been made to point out that Gandhi's constructive programmes have been successfully experimented in the province of Bihar. The national movement in the context of constructive programmes of Gandhi has not been properly analysed in these works.

An attempt has been made to study the subject under the following chapters. In the first chapter a detailed analysis has been made with regard to the production and use of Khadi in the province of Bihar, which formed the main plank of the constructive programmes of Gandhi. Through these weapons Gandhi intended to encourage the people to wear cloths woven by the Indian weavers, and at the same time discourage them from using foreign manufactured goods. In the second chapter, it has been pointed out that a number of national educational institutions sprang up in the province on account of the efforts of local and national leaders and these institutions instilled into the minds of the people ideas of patriotism and nationalism. In the third chapter a detailed analysis has been made with regard to the establishment of Panchayats and arbitration courts in the different parts of the province, and people were encouraged to solve their disputes in these popular courts instead of the courts established by the British rulers. In the fourth chapter, an analysis has been made how through the constructive programmes of Gandhi, the organisation of the Congress was organised and consolidated on sound basis. In the fifth chapter, an attempt has been made to point out the different measures taken by the local and national leaders of the Congress for promoting communal harmony in the province. In the sixth chapter, the most important programme of Gandhi relating to the removal of untouchability has been discussed. Lastly, the chapter 'Conclusion' is concerned with the summary of all the chapters on the basis of discussion and analysis of the problem.

The study is based on records preserved in the State Archives, Government of Bihar, Patna, National Archives, New Delhi and National Library, Calcutta. I have also tried my best to incorporate relevant materials gathered from the newspapers, District record offices, Sadaquat Ashram, Patna, Gandhi Sangrahalaya, Patna, Sinha Library, Patna, A.N. Sinha Institute, Patna and other places. In this connection I have not missed consulting the memoirs of the local and national leaders and biographies of the leaders of the period. These sources have been very much helpful in discussing the problem in all its pros and cons.

1

Production and Use of Khadi

The year 1920 marked the beginning of a new phase in the history of the struggle of emancipation from the yoke of alien rule. By inaugurating a new policy of constructive programme[1] and initiating new steps in the life of the common people, the Congress launched a major attack on the economic policy of the British imperialists in India. The Calcutta session of the Indian National Congress (1920) heralded the dawn of a new economic consciousness among the people in general and the Congress workers in particular with regard to the use of khadi and boycott of foreign machine-made goods in India. The Nagpur session of the Indian National Congress fully endorsed the earlier resolution by "making India economically independent and self-contained, by calling upon merchants and traders to carry out a gradual boycott of foreign trade relations to encourage hand-spinning and hand-weaving, and, on that behalf, by having a scheme of economic boycott planned and formulated by a Committee of experts to be nominated by the All-India Congress Committee."[2]

A large number of Bihar delegates attended the Nagpur session of the Congress in 1920 and they returned with a new spirit which found expression in various activities consisting of the changed programmes and principles adopted there.

Volunteers were recruited in different parts[3] of India and the gospel of Swadeshi was preached by them among the masses with great zeal. Deshbandhu C.R. Das addressed two meetings at Patna on the 11 and 14 February 1921. "I cannot", he observed in one of his speeches, "for one moment be in favour of European industrialism at all. I shall not be at all sorry if some of the things that are manufactured in England are not made here. Do what you should do—work a charkha—and you will realise the result...."[4]

The meeting of the All-India Congress was held at Bezwada on 31 March and 1 April 1921. For purely constructive work it passed a resolution asking the people to concentrate on three items. One of them was the introduction in the villages and cities twenty lakhs of charkhas (spinning wheels). This was to be completed by 30 June next and the respective provinces contributed according to the ratio of its population. The ratio fixed for Bihar was 1,88,000.[5]

Gandhiji discovered that not only should cloth be woven on the handloom but it should be spun on the charkha as an ancillary industry in towns and villages; and from 1921 onward Khaddar became the grand uniform of the Indian patriot.[6]

Promptly and enthusiastically Bihar set herself to the task of fulfilling these conditions. On the commencement of the Satyagraha Week on 6 April 1921, Rajendra Prasad observed, "The Congress Committee has laid severe tests and we have to get through it, if we are worth anything. In this province we have to set 2 lakhs of charkha in good working order."[7] He further observed, "during the last war India had contributed 150 crores to England in order to defeat Germany. Now he wanted only one crore of them to secure Swaraj. If they remember charkha, they would find that it did them no harm. If 50 lakhs of charkha were worked daily, they would be able to save an annual drain of 60 to 70 crores of rupees. They should realise the importance of charkha. During the Satyagraha Week Bihar introduced many charkhas for khadi work."[8]

The Indian National Congress continued to lay stress on constructive activities. The All-India Congress Committee, the first to be elected according to the new constitution, meeting at Bombay on 28, 29 and 30 July 1921, passed a resolution for concentrating attention "upon attaining complete boycott of foreign cloth by the 30th September next and on manufacture of Khaddar by stimulating hand-spinning and hand-weaving."[9] Mahatma Gandhi convened a meeting of the leaders at Bombay on 4 October 1921. A manifesto was issued at this meeting and was endorsed by the All-India Congress Committee on the 15th October.

Copies of this manifesto and of the Delhi Fatwa were circulated in Bihar, and, as in the other parts, Bihar indeed was forging ahead in this fight for freedom on the path chalked out by the Indian National Congress. Constructive activities were pushed on with accelerated speed in the teeth of Governmental opposition and systematic efforts were made to foster the use of Swadeshi clothes and charkha. "Forty-eight depots were opened in eleven districts of the province to place cotton and charkha within easy reach of the people. In most districts the sale of swadeshi cloth was reported to have increased considerably...."[10] Sarla Devi visited several districts in the Chhotanagpur Division preaching the cult of khaddar and charkha. The local leaders of Bihar spoke for these at meetings held in different parts of the province during October and November 1921, to propagate the instructions of the leaders.[11]

The 16th Session of the Bihari Students Conference met at Hazaribagh on 5 and 6 October 1921, under the presidentship of Sarla Devi. Resolutions were passed at this conference:

1. Recommending the boycott of Government schools and colleges.
2. Recommending that students should devote at least half an hour every working day and two hours every Sunday to the spinning of yarn.
3. Requiring every student to boycott foreign cloth and use of khaddar only.

Meeting at Delhi on 4 and 5 November 1921, the All-

India Congress Committee authorised "every province, on its own responsibility, to undertake civil disobedience including non-payment of taxes". The conditions were that in the "Event of individual Civil Disobedience the individual must know hand-spinning and must have completely fulfilled that part of the programme which is applicable to him or her, e.g., he or she must have entirely discarded the use of foreign cloth and adopted only hand-spun and hand-woven garments...."[13]

Khadi work in Bihar began from 1921 when the Bihar Provincial Congress Committee got a good amount for it from the Swaraj Fund. But it did not make satisfactory progress for lack of sufficient experience on the part of the workers. With help from Acharya Kripalani, Rambinod Singh did excellent work in this respect independently by starting a khaddar producing centre at Madhubani. Through the recommendation of Acharya Kripalani and consent of Rajendra Prasad, he got for it a substantial amount as loan from the Khaddar Board.[14] After the formation of All-India Spinners' Association and a branch of it in Bihar with Rajendra Prasad as its Bihar agent and Lakshmi Narayan as its secretary, khadi work was recognized here on new lines, resulting in greater produce and sale of khadi. Under Rajendra Prasad's close supervision khadi work progressed henceforth both quantitatively and qualitatively, and Bihar produced very cheap khaddar cloths. As Darbhanga district was especially famous for khadi production, the office and chief depot of the Bihar branch of All-India Spinners' Association was shifted from Patna to Muzaffarpur, and again for comparative convenience to Madhubani, where gradually the Charkha Sangh constructed its own building."[15]

At several places in Bihar the constructive items, laid down by the Bardoli resolution, were "being tackled in right earnest". For example, in the Dighwara thana of Saran district there were then about seven thousand spinning wheels and five to six thousand looms in working order. The Gandhi Kutir at Malkachak was doing very useful work under the direction of Ram Vinod Singh. It was in intimate touch with nearly two hundred weavers in the surrounding villages, whom it supplied charkha yarn, and received from them in return the full quantity of khaddar, woven with yarn, after due payment of the stipulated wages. The Gandhi Kutir also gave much impetus to spinning, as the poor women of the villages found a ready market here for their yarn. Every spinner got at least seven rupees a month, and this became a means of livelihood, especially to the helpless widows.[16]

Weaving was done by professional weavers although in certain areas in the district of Saran villagers were themselves taking to weaving hand-spun yarn. There were Congress Production Centres at Goran, Hajipur in Muzaffarpur district, Pandaul in Darbhanga district and Dhaka in Champaran district.[17]

The meeting of the Provincial Congress Committee was held at Patna on 5 January 1922, in the light of Ahmedabad resolution. "In order to start civil disobedience in the district or Tehsil, swadeshi should have been fully popularised and the majority of the inhabitants of that area should have begun to use hand-woven and hand-spun cloths. In order to fulfil the object the people should encourage others to use charkha to weave cloth and wear khaddar so that this object might be achieved as soon as possible."[18]

The Bardoli Congress of 11 and 12 February 1922 directed the Congress Organisation to concentrate on the constructive activities like stimulating the use of spinning wheel and manufacture of hand-spun and hand-woven khadi. The All-India Congress Committee from March 10 to 11, 1923, instructed the Congress workers to make intensive efforts to popularise the cult of khaddar.[19] Before the close of the year 1923 the different political bodies emphasised on constructive work. An All-India Khaddar Board was formed, with Jamnalal Bajaj as its Chairman "to organise and carry on khaddar work throughout India under the supervision of the All-India Congress Committee."[20]

The Working Committee and the All-India Khaddar Board had issued an appeal for a supreme effort to make every man and woman in the country wear khadi. The appeal stated:

> "The work before us is of a two-fold nature, we have in the first place to carry on vigorous propaganda to make the people realise to the fullest extent the political significance of khadi work by showing on the one hand, how khadi alone can help to bring about a speedy and effective boycott of piece-goods resulting in the economic freedom of this country, and on the other hand, how it can help us to build up a network of organisation throughout the length and breadth of the country enabling us to offer concerted and disciplined Satyagraha for the attainment cf our goal."[21]

The Provincial Congress Committee meeting was presided over by Maulana Mazharul Haque, which formed a Provincial Khaddar Board with following persons in the year 1924:[22]

1. M. Khurshed Hasnain
2. Anugrah Narayan Sinha
3. Lakshmi Narayan
4. Brij Nath Das
5. Ram Govind Sinha

Khaddar sale went on quite well in this province from January to June. In July, August, September the sale was dull and a good amount of money was required to be kept locked up in stocking cloth. There were selling depots at Muzaffarpur, Hajipur and Patna. Patna depot sold khadi worth Rs. 83,000 upto 31.2.1923. From September 1921, Muzaffarpur sold khadi upto 31.2.1923 worth Rs. 4,34,353 inclusive of whole state.[23]

After the three-day session of the All-India Congress Committee at Ahmedabad from 27 June 1924, Mahatma Gandhi decided to keep himself in the background and to concentrate intensively on constructive work, particularly hand-spinning and hand-weaving.[24] Regarding the future course of action an agreement known as Calcutta Pact arrived on 6 November 1924 with the signature of Mahatma Gandhi, Deshbandhu C.R. Das and Pandit Moti Lal Nehru. It ran as follows:

> "The Congress resolved that different classes of work of the Congress may be done, as may be found necessary, by the different sections within the Congress and that the spread of hand-spinning, hand-weaving and all the antecedent progress and the spread of hand-spun and hand-woven khadi should be carried on."[25]

Spread of khadi work in Bihar in 1924 also deserves special notice. Rajendra Prasad engaged himself intensively in constructive work in Bihar—particularly in national education and the spread of khadi. On the 19th of February 1924, Nilkanth Chatterji moved a resolution in the Bihar and Orissa Legislative Council to the effect that "in all public schools arrangement be made for teaching boys and girls above the age of ten the art of spinning by charkha." Krishna Ballabha Sahay, Jimut Bahan Sen and Dwarka Nath strongly supported it, along with many others, and it was passed.[26] The Congress members elected to the District Boards and Municipalities, tried their best to introduce spinning and khaddar making in schools under their control.[27]

To popularise khadi work, an exhibition was organised at Patna in December 1924 under the guidance of Rajendra Prasad. He made it a purely non-political function, and some government officials participated in it. Prominent among them were Dawson Miller, Chief Justice of the Patna High Court and Hugh Mcpherson, Member of the Governor's Executive Council in Bihar. In the charkha competition during this exhibition, two boys of Malkha-Chauk Gandhi Kutir (Saran) got the first prize. One of them was Satya Narayan Singh. Lady Miller distributed the prizes. In his speech Rajendra Prasad reviewed the progress of khadi work in Bihar till then.[28]

In addressing a preliminary meeting of the Bihari Students' Conference at Patna in April 1924, Rajendra Prasad exhorted the audience to wear Swadeshi cloth and to dedicate themselves to constructive work like spread of khadi.[29]

The period between 1924-28 was a critical phase in the history of Indian nationalism. The period witnessed commencement of communal tension and division among various parties. But there was a silver lining to this thickening cloud gathering over India's political horizon. In fact, during this period of trial for our nationalism, Mahatma Gandhi undertook travels in different parts of the country, preaching with unswerving conviction the supreme efficacy of constructive work of the right type for the country's emancipation from alien rule and internal maladies of diverse kinds.

The All-India Congress Committee, which met at Patna on the 22 and 23 September 1925, passed the resolution as follows:[30]

> "It is resolved that the Congress do now take up and carry on such political work as may be necessary in the interest of the country, and for this purpose do employ the whole of the machinery and funds of the Congress, save and except such funds and assets as are especially earmarked and belonged to the All-India Khaddar Board and Provincial Khaddar Boards, which shall be handed over with all existing financial obligations to the All-India Spinners' Association started by Mahatma Gandhi as an integral part of the Congress Organisation, but with independent existence and full power to administer these funds for fulfilment of its object."

It was now at Patna that the All-India Spinners' Association was born:

> "Whereas the time has arrrived for the establishment of an expert organisation for the development of hand-spinning and khaddar, and whereas experience has shown that such development is not possible without a permanent organisation, unaffected and controlled by politics, political changes or political bodies, an

organisation called the All-India Spinners' Association is hereby established, with the consent of the All-India Congress Committee, as an integral part of the Congress Organisation but with independent existence and powers."[31]

Mahatma Gandhi continued his tour for furtherance of the constructive work among the masses in the interior parts of the country. "I travel", he said, "because I fancy that the masses want to meet me. I centainly want to meet them. I deliver my simple message to them in a few words and they and I are satisfied. It penetrates the mass mind slowly but surely."[32]

Mahatma Gandhi's Bihar trip this time began with his attending the Bihar Provincial Conference at Purulia in September 1925. In the same pandal an industrial exhibition was arranged carefully, and one could see there, as Mahatma Gandhi noted, "Undoubted evolution of Khaddar."[33] He was taken to a village Golunda, a cooperative centre of spinning. He considered it to be an "interesting experiment", calculated to produce good results.[34]

From Purulia Mahatma entered into the area inhabited by the Ho's, the Mundas and the other Adivasi Tribes. "Among these tribes", Mahatma Gandhi recorded, "there is quite a colony of them called Bhaktas, literally meaning devotees. They are believers in khaddar. Men as well as women ply the charkha regularly. They wear khaddar woven by themselves. Many of them had walked miles with their charkhas on their shoulders. I saw nearly four hundred of them all plying their charkhas most assiduously at the meeting I had the privilege of addressing. They have their own Bhajans which they sing in chorus."[35]

From there Mahatma Gandhi was taken to the village of Golkunda, where an experiment in hand-spinning was being made through cooperative society by Girish Chandra Mazumdar, "a khaddar enthusiast". He then motored to Hazaribagh, where he addressed the students of the St. Columbas College. He impressed upon them the dignity of social service through the spinning wheel and khaddar and sincere contact with the village folk."[36]

From Hazaribagh Mahatma Gandhi proceeded to Patna. Here the main work was the activity of the All-India Congress Committee at Patna and the inauguration of the All-India Spinners' Association."[37]

Next Mahatma Gandhi went to Deoghar-Baidyanath Dham and attended the public meeting there. He heard about the terrible suffering of the people of the district in 1921-22 and advised that "there should be persistent agitation among Santhals against the drinking habit and the charkha work should be systematically organised." The total collection throughout his Bihar tour then amounted to 50,000 rupees. A portion of it was added to the capital of the All-India Spinners' Association.[38]

During the first half of January 1925, the Vice-Chairman of the Chhapra Local Board directed sixty to seventy Gurus (teachers) serving under the Board to use charkha, to teach its use to their pupil and wear khaddar.[39]

In February 1925, a Bihar correspondent wrote to Mahatma Gandhi as follows about progress of khadi work in Bihar till then. "There was a meeting of the Bihar Pradesh Congress Committee on January 25. The majority members registered themselves as self spinning members. And the workers from different districts undertook to secure at least 13,000 self:spinning members. It is expected that sufficient cotton will be collected as a donation for supplying to self-spinning members, who cannot afford to find their own cotton. During my peregrination I have noticed that the quality of yarn and khaddar has steadily improved and centralisation through the Khaddar Board has ensured comparatively greater efficiency and accuracy. The following are the production centres with the average monthly output marked against them:

Pandol (Pandaul)	Rs. 3,000
Garol (Goraul)	Rs. 1,500
Hazipur	Rs. 500

There are three selling depots as follows:

Muzaffarpur	Rs. 2,500
Hazipur	Rs. 500
Patna	Rs. 2,000

Thus, it shows the sale balance of the production. But this is not all the production, not all the consumption. There are many spinners who spin to clothe themselves. Though I have no statistics to show the quantity of yarn thus spun and khaddar woven, there must be hundreds who are clothing themselves in this manner. The Gandhi Ashram is a model centre for spinning. I was surprised to notice the wonderful way in which the lads aged 12 were working here. They not only card and spin well but also receive yarn from spinners on hire, test the yarn, pay them wages and take the yarn to the weavers. They can do all these works efficiently and methodically. The quality of its khaddar shows clear improvement upon 1922. The Ashram had the following producing centres:

Madhubani	Rs. 7,000
Malkachak	Rs. 600
Madhupur	Rs. 600

The following were the sale depots:

Madhubani	Rs. 1,500
Bhagalpur	Rs. 1,100
Malkachak	Rs. 500
Jamui	Rs. 500

The Pradesh Congress Committee proposes this year to produce khaddar worth at least five lakhs of rupees. The present monthly production is Rs. 13,000. If they are to manufacture five lakhs, the monthly production must be trebled. Rajendra Prasad is enthusiastic about it. The natural facilities in Bihar are great. I should not, therefore, wonder if the programme is carried out. The people here are anxiously looking forward to your visit. If you can come, the work will certainly receive a great push."[40]

Between January 1925 and January 1926 the total amount of white khadi produced in Darbhanga district was 91,986 yards on which the weaving charges amounted to Rs. 11,604 and the spinning wages came approximately to Rs. 10,203. There were a large number of weavers in the locality and to supply them yarn to the Pandaul production depot started three yarn exchange centres. In the reports of the Bihar Branch of the A.I.S.A. for the year ending September 1926, sent by Rajendra Prasad to Mahatma Gandhi, we get the following information about the progress of khadi work since the work was centralised under the Khadi Board and later under the A.I.S.A.[41]

(*In rupees*)

	April 1924 to Sept. 1924	*Oct. 1924 to Mar. 1925*	*Apr. '24 to Sept. '25*	*Oct. '25 to Mar. '26*	*Apr. '26 to Sep. '26*
Production	21,588	35,273	47,031	51,080	96,723
Sale	17,478	27,784	33,335	51,865	59,678

The foregoing statement did not "include the figures for production and sale of khaddar by the Gandhi Kutir whose work till the beginning of 1926 was on a more extensive scale than of the Provincial Khaddar Board and, latterly, the Bihar Branch of the A.I.S.A." There were eight production and sale centres and eleven sale depots. Besides these there were sale agencies at six places and more were being established. The agency had sixty-five whole-time workers. Their average earnings were Rs. 25 a month. During the year under review 2,698 spinners earned Rs. 29,519; 489 weavers Rs. 36,862; 6 tailors Rs. 230 during two months; 8 dyers and printers Rs. 2,273 including the cost of dye (during six months) and 40 washermen Rs. 1,951 during six months. The spinners and weavers worked only during their spare time and irregularly.[42] According to this report the progress was "not only in regard to increased production and sale but also in regard to this quality of khaddar and reduction in its price." In 1923 the average price was Rs. 1-0-5 pies per yard of fine cloth. In 1926 it was reduced to 13 annas. When the yarn was weak, the weaving charge per yard of 5 inches width was 3 annas 3 pies. On the improvement of the yarn it was reduced to 2 annas 3 pies per yard of the same width. There was no difficulty about getting sufficient numbers of weavers to weave hand-spun yarn. Some of these weavers could weave upto 72 inches width and produced variety of cloths including twills, coatings of various designs, etc. A graduate of the Bihar Vidyapith was incharge of developing dying and printing. The report also contained pregnant reflections on the utility of charkha as a subsidiary industry to supplement the major income of the vast body of poor agricultural population, and on the model of India's old economy which was marked by a fair co-ordination between agriculture and industries conducive to the economic welfare of the country as a whole. An appeal was made through it to the public for the purchase of khaddar.[43]

The period from October 1926 to September 1927 opened with large stock of khadi in stores[44] at different places in Bihar which reduced the liquid capital in the hands of the workers and necessitated the curtailment of the production. Difficulties were experienced in restarting the charkhas which had been stopped for inability of the workers to take the yarn and these were aggravated to a certain extent as a result of Hindu-Muslim riots which had unfortunately taken place last year in the district of Darbhanga, the area where the largest number of khadi production centres were situated and which supplied the bulk of yarn required for it. But Mahatma Gandhi's tour gave considerable impetus to khadi work.

Besides speaking in large gatherings on the utility of khadi, desirability of removing untouchability and other cognate subjects, he also hawked khadi in these public meetings. This enhanced the demand for khadi; and not only was accumulated stock cleared but several depots began to have increased sale.[45] To make khadi available to the people both in the urban and rural area, hawking was resorted to by others also and between 1 October 1926 and the end of September 1927, khadi worth Rs. 5,273 was sold through hawking in some of the villages and the towns.[46]

It should be noted that to popularise khadi, exhibitions were held in 1926 at different centres in the province under the guidance of Rajendra Prasad. The first one was opened by Satish Chandra Dasgupta of the Khadi Pratisthan, Calcutta, on the grounds of the Bihar Vidyapith. The second one was held in the Bihar Youngmen's Institute, Patna, by Sadhu Baswani of Sindh. The third one was organised at Arrah, the fourth one was opened at Muzaffarpur by Maulvi Mohammad Safi and fifth one was opened at Chhapra by Mazharul Haque. The sixth one was held at Mairwa, a small village in the district Chhapra and the seventh one at Gaya on 11 June 1926. Khadi exhibitions were arranged at some other places too. Khadi was hawked and sold at these exhibitions and magic-lantern lectures delivered in the evenings illustrating the khadi movement. These exhibitions were visited by "Congressmen, Non-Congressmen, Government officials, Zamindars, Lawyers, big and small merchants and in some cases even Europeans."[47]

A khadi exhibition at Bettiah was opened in uly 1926 by Dr. H.C. Prior, who had succeeded Rutherford as Manager of the Bettiah Raj. Another exhibition at Motihari was inaugurated by a famous Christian Missionary, named J.Z. Hodge. At Bettiah and Motihari exhibitions the sale amounted to Rs. 1,304-12-3 and Rs. 1,162 8 annas 9 pies respectively.[48]

At Jamshedpur the khadi exhibition was opened by a highly placed officer of Tata & Company, Mr. Temple, who was himself an engineer and Administrator of the Jamshedpur town. Mr. Kenan, General Manager of Tata & Company and his wife, both of whom were Americans, visited the exhibition as was done by some other high officers too. There was a good sale of khadi at this exhibition.[49]

In August 1926, one exhibition was held at Laheriasarai, Darbhanga, its opening ceremony having been performed by Rajendra Prasad and another exhibition was inaugurated in the same month at Deoghar by Seth Jamna Lal Bajaj. The sale of these two exhibitions amounted to Rs. 1,445-15-6 and Rs. 159-8-6 respectively.[50]

The 13th Bihar Khadi exhibition was held at Hazaribagh from 14 to 16 August 1926 and this too was opened by Rajendra Prasad. Sale at this exhibition amounted to Rs. 3,010-2-0 and the number of purchasers was 620. B.F. Bharucha of Bombay was present at this function. Kharag Babu and Hem Babu, Professors of Philosophy and Chemistry respectively of the Saint Columbas College, rendered much help to make the exhibition a success.[51]

At Ranchi the khadi exhibition was opened in presence of Rajendra Prasad, by S.K. Sahay at 4 P.M. on 5 October 1926, in the Ranchi Arya Samaj Hall. Some Tana Bhagats attended it.[52]

The local Non-Cooperation leaders of Ranchi, namely, P.C. Mitra, Deoki Nandan Lal, Rama Nand Brahmachari and some others were indefatigably exerting for furtherance of constructive national works. On 12 March 1926, they held a meeting at Ranchi and exhorted the audience to carry on such works undauntedly.[53] They celebrated the national week from 6, April to 13 April 1926, by starting with a procession, which included a large number of Tana Bhagats and addressing meetings. Ram Narayan Singh, President of the Hazaribagh Congress Committee, also spoke in one of these meetings. A charkha demonstration was organised in front of the Durga Mandap where Mahendra Prasad of Chhapra, who had then come to Ranchi appealing for Hindu-Muslim unity and spread of khadi work.[54] Thus, in spite of the formal suspension of the Non-cooperation Movement, constructive activities were vigorously continued in this province.

Mahatma Gandhi's second Bihar tour in this period began from 11 January 1927. To those who came to receive him at railway station in Bihar, he spoke in one minute speech, "I have come here to do business, to collect money for charkha and khadi and to sell khadi. Who knows this it may be my last visit to Bihar! Let me do as much business as I can."[55] Starting from Daltonganj he went to Gaya. He crossed the Ganges at Patna and reached Muzaffarpur on 27 January 1927. In the afternoon that day he addressed a crowded meeting in the Tilak Maidan there. At Muzaffarpur the students surrounded Mahatma Gandhi, who began to speak to them by narrating one of the sweetest memories of Champaran: "You students, I wonder if there is still any one of those old boys at college with Kripalani at their head were the first to welcome and harbour me in Champaran. Your response during the year that followed was no less remarkable. Will you not do today the little that I am asking of you ?" He advised them for khadi wearing and Brahmacharya.[56]

In the night Mahatma Gandhi started for Motihari with his party, consisting of Rajendra Prasad, Mahadev Desai, Kasturbai and Parvati (wife of Jai Prakash Narayan).[57] At Motihari, collections were not good "because of the faulty management of the meetings" there.[58] Passing across the rich alluvial tracts of the Chhapra district, Mahatma Gandhi spent one quite day at Jiradei, which he considered to be "a place of pilgrimage" as the birth-place of Rajendra Prasad.[59] Then moving through some other subdivisions in Chhapra district, "Studded at a very half-at-mile ameralds of mangogroves and carpeted with fields smiling with green tuar and wheat and gram and peas".[60] He went again to east and north of Darbhanga.

During his tour, Mahatma Gandhi also began the novel practice of taking some quantity of khadi with himself and selling it at every meeting and every station. Because of its khadi depots, the district of Darbhanga was considered by the party of Mahatma Gandhi to be "the land of tirthas" (centre of pilgrimage).[61] "The visit (to them)", writes Mahadev Desai, "was not only a study, but a revelation, a feast for the eyes and a solace for the soul. Pandaul and Madhubani and Sakari and Kapasi conjure up visions before you. In beautifully swept courtyards those young women were sitting—all mussalmans, it will gladden Maulana Shaukat Ali's heart to know working out their wheels a music of which the echoes still resound in the ears. Not ten or fifty, but three hundred giving as wonderful demonstration of the art of which they were born.[62] At Belwar there was a colony of Brahmin women spinners, girls spinning on their nice little taklies and elderly women on their wheels. At Kapasia "A Mussalman village organised by Hindu youths", "nearly all the weavers were found weaving hand-spun yarn."[63]

At Gaya, the Municipality presented an address to Mahatma Gandhi which was sceptical about khadi and untouchability programme. At Gaya, again, the Hindu Sabha gave an address to him, which besides expressing heartiest sympathy with khadi.[64]

The last day of Mahatma Gandhi's Bihar tour of this time was given to the students and Professors of the Vidyapith and to the khadi workers. The authorities of the Vidyapith organised a khadi exhibition at the same time. It was opened by Satish Chandra Dasgupta of Khadi Pratisthan, Calcutta, who delivered a speech[65] emphasising the importance of charkha and khaddar for solution of India's poverty and independence. He paid eloquent testimony to the work of the Khadi Centres in Bihar itself, which had been organised mainly by Rajendra Prasad and Ram Binod Singh. In conclusion he observed:

> "If we could attain Swaraj through the spinning wheel it would demonstrate better than anything else that love is mightier than force. Let India's hungry millions be fed. Let her honour be restored and then she would be able to give to the world one of the greatest spiritual teachings that the power of love is greater than that of brute force. Gandhiji has said that his political work is nothing to him as compared with his spiritual work. It is not his way to talk in superlatives. He means what he says. In our impatience to attain swaraj without any effort we may not understand the significance of what he says, but if simply work on for the economic salvation

of India by spinning and weaving khaddar, the field may be prepared for the realisation of the higher and nobler aspect of the movement."

Mahatma Gandhi addressed the Convocation of the Bihar Vidyapith in 1927. On this occasion he stated, "The charkha should be the very pivot and centre of all works in national institutions." He further expressed, "Let the Snatakas take their degrees, learn anything they like, but let it centre round the charkha, let their economics and their science subserve the purpose of charkha. Do not relegate the charkha to an old corner. The charkha is the sun of the solar system of our activities. Without it Vidyapiths are Vidyapiths in name. Lord Irwin told God's truth, when he said, that for any advancement through the Councils we should look to the British Parliament. Let us not be angry with him. He cannot think but in terms of the Parliament. The sun of his system is London, the sun of our system is the charkha. I may be mistaken in this, but, so far as I am not convinced of the mistake, I shall treasure it. The charkha at any rate is incapable of harming anybody and without it we, and if I may say so, even the world, will go to rack and ruin. We know what Europe has been feeling after the war in which lies were propagated as the highest religion. The world is weary of the after-effects of the war and even as the charkha is India's comforter today, it may be the world's tomorrow, because it stands not for the greatest number but for the greatest good for all. Whenever I see an erring man, I say to myself I have also erred; when I see a lustful man, I say to myself so I was once; and in this way I feel kinship with everyone in the world, and feel that I cannot be happy without the humblest being happy. It is in this sense that I want you to make the charkha the centre of your studies. Just as Prahalada saw Ram everywhere and Tulsidas could see nothing but Rama even in image of Krishna, let all your learning be directed to realising the implications of the charkha. Our science, our carpentry, our economics should all be utilised for making the charkha the prop and mainstay of our poorest. I know in Gujrat Vidyapith we have not yet succeeded in doing it, you are not doing it. I am not saying this in a spirit of complaint. I am simply pouring out the agony of my heart. May you all understand it."[66]

Mahatma Gandhi met the Khadi workers also on the last date of his tour in Bihar. Rajendra Prasad arranged on this occasion a special khadi exhibition in the Sinha Institute, a notable gift of S. Sinha, father of modern Bihar, to this State, a large crowd rushed on the spot over which a shamiana had been erected. In a talk in Hindi, Mahatma Gandhi read out before the audience, the charts of daily income per head in different countries of the world and of production and sale of khadi during recent year prepared by the students of Vidyapith. This production meant Rs. 30,000. Rs. 3,000 distributed to the poor women of Bihar. Referring the scanty income of the vast majority of India's poor people, he observed:

> "As a result of hard thinking and living contact with millions during recent years I have suggested the charkhas as the only means calculated to supplement this income." Owing to tremendous rush, the ministers, some barristers and government officials whom Rajendra Prasad had invited to the function, attended it next day, and in one day and half over Rs. 2,000 worth of khaddar was sold.[67]

The Congress, at its Calcutta Session of 29 December 1928, passed a resolution outlining future programme of constructive works for Congressmen, in the legislature and outside. Such works were prohibition of drinks and intoxicating drugs, boycott of foreign cloth by advancing and stimulating production of hand-spun and hand-woven khaddar.

According to a resolution of the meeting of the working Committee of the Congress held in Calcutta on 3 January 1929, Mahatma Gandhi prepared a scheme for the boycott of foreign cloth through khadi. Meeting at Delhi on the 17 and 19 February 1929, the Working Committe adopted this scheme, the chief features of which were as follows:

"1. Congress organisation should call for volunteers, men and women, to go from door to door in every town and village having a Congress Committee and collect foreign cloth in the possession of the householder and deliver or receive orders for khadi required by such householders.

2. All khadi so supplied should bear the stamp of the All-India Spinners' Association and price should be distinctly marked on them.

3. Voluntary preachers should be called for to popularise the use of khadi and to advocate complete boycott of foreign cloth.

4. Resolution should be moved in the Provincial Legislature as well as the Central, calling upon their cloth purchasers in khadi irrespective of its so-called costliness."[68]

Mahatma Gandhi arranged a cloth burning demonstration in Calcutta on the 14th March 1929. During this time in Bihar special efforts were made to push up both production and sale of khadi. Some new centres of production were opened and the old ones were developed. Among the new centres opened special mention may be made of Kishunganj in Purnea and Amarpur in Bhagalpur for their showing good results.[69]

On the 15th of May 1929, a meeting attended by about three hundred people was held at Kateyan (close to the Bazar Saran) where there was organised mela, Pandit Girish Tiwary appealed for the use of khaddar and regretted its non-use by audience. Adya Saran Pandey explained that man did not command respect unless he had a good home, good cloth and good food.[70]

The Bihar Youth Conference met at Monghyr on 12 December 1929. In the absence of Subhash Chandra Bose, Pandit Prajapati Mishra presided. He spoke with great emphasis on the use of khaddar by youngmen.[71]

In Bihar the Provincial Congress Committee issued[72] on 20 January 1930, the following programme for the celebration of the independence day on 26 January next:

1. The national flag should be hoisted exactly at 8 in the morning at the place where meeting is to be held. In the evening the flag should be taken down only when the meeting is over.
2. After the flag is hoisted in the morning the public should busy themselves with either of the following works and should not waste even a minute of their time:

(a) As many as possible, houses should be visited and Congress resolution explained to the people and members enrolled for the year 1930.

(b) Hawking of khaddar.

(c) Charkha spinning.

(d) Enrolment of volunteers. They should be habitual weavers of khadi and should have signed the Congress pledge."

On 15 July 1930, Pandit Bedverta addressed a meeting at Khodaibagh, Police Station Chhapra, and asked the audience to use khadi, enlist themselves as volunteers.[73] On 21 July 1930, a meeting was held at Pachrukhi, Police Station Siwan, and the importance of the use of khaddar was stressed.[74]

In September 1930, on the constructive side, the "Swadeshi Week" was observed at Ranchi in which two days were specially devoted to charkha and takali competitions. One day was reserved for the males and another for the females. The aboriginal, both males and females, enthusiastically participated in these competitions. Such competitions were held at other places too, such as, at Deoghar, Sasaram and Patna City. One Khadi Board was established at Deoghar to organise production of khadi there and a Mahila Sabha with about 100 ladies as its members, was also formed at this place.[75]

Side by side with movement for the boycott of foreign cloth, charkha and khaddar was also gaining ground every day. The output of hand-spun yarn increased considerably in the province. The people had taken to spinning in large number and enquiries were pouring in as to what they should do with their yarn. In the Santhal Parganas the output of yarn had gone up to 100 maunds every month. In the jurisdiction of Ekma thana in the district of Saran, the number of charkhas working regularly was 237 while in Guthani thana there were 2,997 charkhas and 50 looms working. In Barahia thana in the district of Monghyr, the number of charkbas had gone up to 300.[76]

The output of khadi was ever on increase. This work was being pushed forward vigorously by holding charkha and takali competition at various places. Spinning and carding exhibitions were held at several places in Darbhanga and other districts on the occasion of the visit of Jamna Lal Bajaj and party. Charkha and takali spinning was increasing by leaps and bounds in Bishunpur, Dumar and other places in the district of Purnea and in the villages in the jurisdiction of Sonepur and Kothianaraon in the district of Saran. About 500 charkhas were plying regularly in Gauripur-Bikram Circle, in the district of Bhagalpur.[77]

Under the auspices of the Muzaffarpur District Congress Committee the National Week was fifingly celebrated. A mass meeting was held on the evening of 13 March 1931 and there was also an exhibition of khadi and spinning competition. The fourth session of the Manbhum District Congress Committee held on 25 and 26 April 1931. Arrangement had been made for a Charkha and Khaddar exhibition.[78]

The following resolutions were adopted at the last Working Committee meeting held at Sadakat Ashram, Patna on 20 April 1931:

"(i) As the growth of khaddar spinning and weaving was not satisfactory owing to the stoppage of Charkha and non-purchase of yarn in areas not controlled by Charkha Sangh and as Khaddar occupies a very important place in the means of boycott of foreign cloth, it is necessary in the opinion of this committee that independent arrangement on behalf of the Congress Committee be made to organise Khadi work with a view to making areas self-sufficient in the matter of cloth. The

Congress Committee and Charkha Sangh should co-operate with each other in organising this work of self-sufficiency.

(ii) The subordinate Committees of the Congress are instructed to appoint capable workers under the organisation.

(iii) The Committee notes with surprise and pain that the Provincial Charkha Sangh has got an accounted stock of khadi. For immediate sale of khadi, which is necessary, it requests the subordinate Committees to correspond with the Charkha Sangh.

(iv) The Secretary of the Bihar Provincial Congress Committee is authorised to appoint a worker for compilation of history of the Civil Disobedience Movement in the Province.

(v) That a worker training class be opened in Bihar Vidyapith."[79]

It had been decided to hold Bihar Provincial Khadi Exhibition at Patna from 26 July to 1 August 1931. The following items were to be exhibited at the exhibition and people throughout the Province were invited to send in exhibits to the Manager, Khadi Bhandar, Bakarganj, Patna. Best of exhibits to be exhibited at this exhibition were:

"1. Kapas from different parts of the province with full description.
2. Cotton produced in different parts of the Province.
3. Hand-spun yarn on charkhas and takali.
4. Khadi produced locally out of hand-spun yarn.
5. Hand gins.
6. Carding bow locally used along with tant.
7. Spinning wheels and takali used locally.
8. Hand-spun yarn produced during the recent incarnation of Congress workers.

9. Hand-spun and hand-moven cloth of antiquities is about 100 or 50 years old.
10. Durries and carpets, etc."[80]

In view of the removal of the ban on the Congress organisation, the Working Committee meeting at Wardha from 12 to 13 June 1934, advised responsible Congress workers to expedite the re-organisation of Congress Committee within respective jurisdictions and engage Congressmen in constructive activities, such as, production of khaddar.[81]

Besides being busy for election, the Congress members also engaged themselves in various constructive activities during 1935. Many Provincial Congress Workers joined Mahatma Gandhi's All-India Spinners' Association and began work at several centres. In the month of September 1935, the Village Industry's Association in Aurangabad subdivision induced a zamindar to give them ten bighas of land for opening a free dispensary, a spinning school and a library.[82] In Muzaffarpur district persons like Ram Charan Singh, Janakdhari Prasad and Lakshmi Narayan, Secretary, All-India Spinners' Association, devoted themselves whole-heartedly to implement the programme of the Association above-mentioned.[83]

The Barh Local Board in its meeting held on 25 October 1937, by a resolution resolved that charkhas be supplied to all the primary schools and the teachers be directed to learn its use and popularise khadi among the boys.[84]

A Charkha Centre under the presidentship of Deonarayan Lal, a Congress worker of Charkha Sangh, had been formed which was making steady progress. Deonarayan Lal, through the help of Bhawani Babu of Bedaul Charkha Sangh, started the work of spinning by supplying charkhas and other necessary materials. The work had since been going on in full swing and a large number of charkhas were working regularly. Every possible help was being rendered by Shivashray Prasad, a prominent member of the Tirhut Seva Sangh to push on the work.[85]

Jaglal Chaudhary, Minister of Excise and Health paid a visit to Bihar Town High English School on 17 April 1938. He visited the charkha class recently started at the school and was glad at the move of the school authority. Chaudhary suggested to the headmaster to send some teachers and boys to him for instruction and advised him to get charkha made by Charkha Sangh. It was nice to see the Minister seated on a carpet by Charkha Sangh.[86]

The Secretary of the Bihar Provincial Congress Committee had addressed a letter to Pattabhi Sitaramayya inviting him to open the khadi exhibition which was to be held at Patna on the occasion of 69th birth anniversary of Mahatma Gandhi. The Khadi Week was to be celebrated from 21st instant.[87]

Mohammd Ashique, President, Gaya Muslim League and Latifur Rahman, M.L.A., addressed Mussalmans of Rafiganj thana on 23 October 1938. Shah Moiuddin Ahmad presided.

Latifur Rahman referred to the Karachi Resolution of the Muslim League about khaddar and exhorted the audience to use khaddar prepared by Momins on the occasion of Idul-Fitra.[88]

The Bihar Provincial Congress Working Committee met at Patna on 17 and 18 December 1938. A resolution relating to advisability of taking disciplinary action by Congress against offenders against the principles of the Sati and use of certified khadi forwarded by the Secretary, Bihar Branch of the All-India Spinners' Association was considered by the Committee and after discussion it was decided to forward it to Mahatma Gandhi for his advice.[89]

Brij Kishore Prasad Sahay, Incharge of Sales and Propaganda of the All-India Spinners' Association, Bihar Branch, wrote:

> "The following were the comparative figures of khadi production and sale in the first half of the year 1938-39:

Production of cloth by weight	3,205 mds.—4,259 mds.
Total sale	Rs. 2,87,287—4,50,360"

The figures published above give an idea regarding the work done by the All-India Spinners' Association, Bihar Branch during six months ending June 30, 1939, as also an idea for the corresponding period of 1938. Yarn production had been curtailed in 1939 owing to a huge supply of stock at the end of the year 1939. Thus, we find that sale of goods produced by All-India Spinners' Association, Bihar Branch comes to Rs. 41,000 at the end of the year 1938.[90]

Lakshmi Narayan, Secretary, All-India Spinners' Association, Bihar Branch, wrote that the Khadi exhibition being held in the premises of the Old Pirbahor Police Station near the Civil Court was attracting a good number of customers every evening. It had been decided to sell a part of the evening of Tuesday, October 10, from 6 P.M. to 9 P.M. for ladies exclusively.[91]

The All-India Spinners' Association, Bihar Branch, celebrated Gandhiji's 71st Birth Day between the 2nd October and 23rd October by making arrangement for sale of khadi on an extensive scale throughout the State. Khadi Hundies were introduced for the first time in the Province. The sale of khadi and khadi hundies during the celebration exceeded a lakh of rupees.[92]

At Sonepur Fair, the Khadi Exhibition organised by the Madhubani Branch of All-India Spinners' Association was opened by L.N. Singh. The sale of khadi was very satisfactory.[93]

Thus, during the period under review, Khadi work in Bihar progressed both qualitatively and quantitatively. Khadi and charkha became the symbol of the Congress. Not only the Congressmen but people as well found pride and glory in using hand-spun and hand-woven khaddar. All sections of society responded enthusiastically to Mahatma Gandhi's call to produce and use khaddar.

References

1. Sitaramayya, B. Pattabhi, *History of the Indian National Congress*, Vol. I, p. 207.
2. Datta, K.K., *History of the Freedom Movement in Bihar*, Vol. I, p. 317.
3. *The Non-Cooperation and Khilafat Movement in Bihar and Orissa*, p. 27.
4. *The Searchlight*, February 15, 1921.
5. Bamford, P.C., *History of the Non-Cooperation and Khilafat Movement*, printed by Government of India in 1925, p. 27.
6. Sitaramayya, B. Pattabhi, *History of the Indian National Congress*, Vol. I, p. 43.
7. *The Searchlight*, April 6, 1921.
8. Prasad, Rajendra, *Mahatma Gandhi and Bihar*, p. 47.
9. Quoted in Datta, K.K., *History of the Freedom Movement in Bihar*, Vol. I, p. 376.
10. *The Non-Cooperation and Khilafat Movement in Bihar and Orissa*, p. 67.
11. For detail, see Ibid, pp. 69-70.
12. Datta, K.K., *History of the Freedom Movement in Bihar*, Vol. I, p. 395.
    The Searchlight, October 8, 1921.
13. Datta, K.K., *History of the Freedom Movement in Bihar*, Vol. I, p. 397.
14. Prasad, Rajendra, *Atmakatha*, pp. 264-65.
15. Ibid., p. 266.
16. Datta, K.K., *History of the Freedom Movement in Bihar*, Vol. I, p. 399.
17. *The Searchlight*, March 7, 1921.
18. *Bihar P.C.C. report for the first half of January* 1922.
19. *The Non-Cooperation Movement in Bihar and Orissa*, p. 129.
20. Datta, K.K., *History of the Freedom Movement in Bihar*, Vol. I, p. 455.
21. *The Searchlight*, February 17, 1924.
22. Ibid., March 7, 1924.
23. Ibid.
24. Prasad, Rajendra, *Atmakatha*, pp. 61-62.

25. Quoted in Datta, K.K., *History of the Freedom Movement in Bihar*, Vol. I, p. 460.
26. *Proceedings of the Bihar and Orissa Legislative Council*, Vol. I, January-February, 1924, pp. 283-332.
27. Prasad, Rajendra, *Atmakatha*, pp. 235-36.
28. Ibid., pp. 242-43.
29. *The Searchlight*, April 11, 1924.
30. *Young India*, 1924-25, p. 564.
31. Ibid., p. 565.
32. Desai, Mahadev, *Gandhiji in Indian Villages*, p. 232.
33. Ibid.
34. Ibid.
35. Ibid., p. 238.
36. Ibid., p. 243.
37. Ibid., p. 244.
38. Ibid., p. 260.
39. *File No. 25 (May) 1924, Home (Political Special) Department*, National Archives of India, New Delhi.
40. *Young India*, February 12, 1925.
41. Datta, K.K., *History of the Freedom Movement in Bihar*, Vol. I, p. 489.
42. *Young India*, 1927-28, p. 49.
43. Ibid.
44. *Vide Appendix XXII*, Datta, K.K., *History of the Freedom Movement in Bihar*, Vol. I.
45. *Young India*, December 22, 1927.
46. Ibid.
47. Ibid., July 1, 1926.
48. Ibid., Aug. 19, 1926.
49. Prasad, Rajendra, *Atmakatha*, pp. 266-67.
50. Ibid., pp. 268-69.
51. *Young India*, September 16, 1926.
52. *Report of the Superintendent of Police, Ranchi*, dated 8.10.1926.
53. Ibid., dated 16.3.1926.
54. Ibid.
55. *Young India*, 1927-28, p. 53.
56. Ibid., p. 78.

57. *Autobiography of Janakdhari Prasad*, p. 144.
58. *Young India*, 1927-28, p. 77.
59. Ibid., p. 53.
60. Ibid.
61. Ibid., 1927-28, p. 74,
62. Ibid.
63. Ibid., p. 76.
64. Ibid., 1927-28, pp. 57-58.
65. Ibid., March 25, 1926.
66. Ibid., 1927-28, pp. 81-84.
67. Ibid., p. 80.
68. Ibid., 1927-28, pp. 81-84.
69. Datta, K.K., *History of the Freedom Movement in Bihar*. Vol. II, p. 15.
70. *Extract from B. & O. Police Abstract of Intelligence*, No. 22, dated June 1, 1929, para 420.
71. *The Searchlight*, December 14, 1929.
72. Ibid., January 22, 1930.
73. *File No. 139(B) 1930, Extract from the Weekly Confidential Diary of the Superintendent of Police, Saran* for the period ending July 23, 1930, Bihar Political Special, Patna.
74. Ibid.
75. Datta, K.K., *History of the Freedom Movement in Bihar*, Vol. II, p. 124.
76. *The Searchlight*, November 14, 1930.
77. Ibid., November 21, 1930.
78. Ibid., April 17, 1931.
79. Ibid., April 25, 1931.
80. Ibid., June 13, 1931.
81. Datta, K.K., *History of the Freedom Movement in Bihar*, Vol. II, p. 230.
82. *Fortnightly report of the Patna Commissioner* for the period ending September 13 and 27, 1935.
83. *The Indian Nation*, October 20, 1935.
84. Ibid., October 28, 1937.
85. Ibid., April 14, 1938.
86. Ibid., April 22, 1938.

87. Ibid., Sept. 6, 1938.
88. Ibid., October 29, 1938.
89. Ibid., December 22, 1938.
90. Ibid., August 27, 1939.
91. Ibid., October 12, 1939.
92. Ibid., October 31, 1939.
93. Ibid., December 9, 1939.

2

Establishment of National Educational Institutions

The response to the Nagpur Congress was noticeable in the field of education. Though the number of Non-cooperators was not large, there was an earnest move towards National Education. Mahatma Gandhi's appeal to the finer instincts of the youth of the country to devote themselves to its service, and to shun the institutions which had been created and maintained to kill all manliness in them, was responded with enthusiasm. None was the work confined merely to boycott. National universities, national colleges and national schools of all grades were started in different parts of the country.[1]

It was under Mahatma Gandhi's influence during his short tour in Bihar in December 1920 and in the beginning of 1921 that some national schools were started here and some existing schools were nationalised by repudiating the affiliation to the university as well as refusing to accept grants-in-aid from the Government,[2] throughout the province. In June 1922 there were 41 High Schools consisting of 4,500 students. The Primary and Middle Schools numbering about six hundred consisted of 17,000 students.[3]

Mahatma Gandhi was decisively in favour of the establishment of a National College (Rashtriya Mahavidyalaya) in Bihar. The local leaders of the new movement were at first vacillating on account of uncertainty of the funds for its maintenance and some of the "senior leaders had all parted company on the question of Non-Cooperation."[4] However, Mahatma Gandhi gave them the much needed impetus by placing at their disposal seven or eight thousand rupees, then collected by him in Bihar,[5] for the purpose of starting the national schools in the province, with the object of providing instruction to the students who gave up studies in the government and government controlled institutions and with a view to provide education on sound lines. The national school was intended to prepare the students for service to the country and to enable them to earn their livelihood[6] through instruction of practical nature. Accordingly the Bihar National College was started on 5 January 1921.[7]

Mahatma Gandhi had come to Bengal and opened the National College on 4 February 1921. He reached Patna in the morning of 6 February accompanied by Kasturbai and Muhammad Ali,[8] and performed on that day the opening ceremony of the National College and of the Bihar Vidyapith.[9] The Bihar Vidyapith was "to co-ordinate the activities of all the national institutions that were spinning up in the Province and to control and guide them."[10] On this occasion Mahatma Gandhi referred to the brotherly cordiality of his two Champaran co-workers, Rajendra Prasad and Brij Kishore Prasad, exhorted the professors to live up to the ideals of the great seers of ancient India, and advised the students to create an example of simple living and high thinking which could be imitated by others. He also announced that during his recent tour of Jharia he collected Rs. 6,000 for the setting up of the National University and this amount was contributed mostly by the Gujratis, Bengalies and Marwaris. A Bengali zamindar of Manbhum district had given him Rs. 2,000 for that purpose. He then went to Dinapur where he opened a national school and on the same day in the afternoon, he opened the Patna City National School.[11]

Mazharul Haque became the Chancellor and Brajkishore Prasad Vice-Chancellor of the Vidyapith and Rajendra Prasad became Principal of the National College. Resigning from their respective posts, Badri Nath Verma of the Department of English, Bihar National College, Jagannath Prasad of the Department of Sanskrit, Patna College, Ram Sundar Bose of the Department of Philosophy, T.N.J. College, Bhagalpur, joined the College as Professors. Jagat Narayan Lal, Ram Charitra Singh and Abdul Bari were also on the teaching staff of this College. On the persuasion of Safi Muhammad Daudi, arrangement was made to examine the students who did not want to appear at the Government College Examination. A Government account mentions that the "Examinations of the national university were held from 14 March 1921, at ten centres in the Province. The matriculation examinations were held at all the centres and the I.A., I.Sc., B.A. and B.Sc. examinations were held at Patna, Bhagalpur, Muzaffarpur and Monghyr. Altogether 387 candidates appeared for the matriculation, 75 for I.A. and I.Sc., 33 for B.A., and 10 for the B.Sc. examinations. Candidates were examined in the courses they were preparing for the government university examinations."[12]

The National College had started with a few students. "Soon afterwards", wrote Rajendra Prasad in 1931, "some of the best students of the university, most of whom were scholarship holders and prizemen, came out of the Government College and marched in a body to the National College where they were welcome by us. We had hardly anything to offer them to compare with what they had left behind except a nobler ideal to work and live for. Some of them stuck to us and are still doing national work. Others, however, worked for a year or more, then went back and some of them are holding responsible posts in government services today."[13]

The Rashtriya Mahavidyalaya was owned by the Rashtriya Shiksha Mandal, which consisted of four categories of members. Persons paying Rs. 5,000 or more in a lump sum became patrons, while those who paid Rs. 500 or more were called donors. A subscriber had to pay Rs. 5 annually, whereas those who had rendered notable service to the cause of national education were entitled to become ordinary members. The Shiksha Mandal regulated and guided the general policy of the institution; and the details of the administration were left in the hands of another body called the College Council of fifteen members, consisting of the Chancellor, the Vice-Chancellor and the Registrar of the Vidyapith, the Principal of the Rashtriya Mahavidyalaya, five members to the college staff and six persons elected by the Rashtriya Shiksha Mandal.[14]

It was a matter of satisfaction that a National School had been opened at Chhapra. Hari Nath Verma, B.A., LL.B., a non-cooperating pleader had been in charge of the school and the management had been entrusted to Mahendra Pr asad and Harihar Saran. It was hoped that the school would work satisfactorily under the able guidance of three gentlemen and there would be no cause of complaint. The guardians of the boys were suggested to patronise the school by sending their wards for education there.[15]

In the Tirhut Division, the Chhapra Collegiate School developed into a national school and "there was considerable unrest in the Greer Bhumihar Brahman Collegiate School at Muzaffarpur."[16] Three or four High English Schools—Muzaffarpur G.B.B. Collegiate, Saraswati Academy (Darbhanga), a School at Gaya and Chhapra Collegiate School—had been nationalised and were being controlled on purely national lines. It should be noted that in all the National Schools that had been started in this Province, there was a very fair number of students on the rolls and the number was increasing. The National College in Patna, that was opened at some time in the early part of January 1921, had since been converted into a University and was arranging to hold examination for non-cooperating students. National schools, both for the primary and secondary stages, came into existence in almost every district, the total number of the two being about 250 and 50 respectively. In all, about 20 to 25 thousand of students began to receive education in these national schools.[18]

A National School was started in Koath, P.S. Bikramganj. Bindyabasini Prasad became the Headmaster, Arrah National School. National schools were soon started also at Gogri (Kharagpur), Khagaria (Begusarai) and Tarapur in Monghyr district. A national school was opened at Daltonganj and the government-aided Sanskrit Telat Hussainabad was transformed into a National Middle School.[19]

Biharsharif quikly responded to the call of Mahatma Gandhi. Owing to the magnificent Trust created by Edal Singh of Ranibigha, the Nalanda College had shortly before brought into existence. A Congress Committee was organised for the first time at Biharsharif with Brij Nandan Prasad as its Secretary. A Khilafat Committee also was constituted. These two bodies decided to start a National School in the town of Biharsharif for the benefit of a large number of students, who had then come out of the college. Apart from general instruction, spinning and weaving formed an important item of training.[20]

The control of education in the national institutions in Bihar was vested in a National Council of Education for Bihar consisting of the following gentlemen[21]:

1. Mazharul Haque
2. Dip Narayan Singh
3. Dharnidhar
4. Maulvi Muhammad Safi
5. Gorakh Prasad
6. Brij Kishore Prasad
7. Qazi Abdul Wadud
8. Pandit Ram Shankar Mishra
9. Qazi Ahmad Husain
10. Maulvi Nazir Ahmad
11. Maulvi Md. Zubair
12. Krishna Prakash Sen Sinha
13. Maulvi Warasat Rasul.

On the teaching staff of the National College at Patna, were:[22]

1. Rajendra Prasad, Principal

2. Badri Nath Verma, M.A. (English), Vice-Principal
3. Prem Sunder Bose, M.A. (Philosophy)
4. Jagat Narayan Lal, M.A. (Economics)
5. Fuldev Sahay Verma, M.Sc. Chemistry)
6. Maulvi Abdul Bari
7. Pandit Ram Nirikshan Singh, M.A. (Sanskrit)
8. Krishna Ballava Sahay, B.A. (Hons.), Gait Gold Medalist.

Some other members of the staff appointed afterwards were:[23]

9. Ram Charitra Singh, M.Sc. (Chemistry)
10. Arunodya Pramanic, M.Sc. (Mathematics)
11. Birendra Nath Sen Gupta, M.A. (History)
12. Janada Prasanha Saha, M.A (Politics)
13. Kashi Nath Prasad, B.Sc. (Hons.)
14. Ram Das Gaur, M.Sc.
15. Maulvi Md. Ozair Munemi (Urdu).

The Bardoli Congress of 11 and 12 February 1922, instructed the Congress organisation to concentrate on the constructive activities like organising national schools. In the year 1924, J.C. Bose came to address that year's convocation of the Patna University, was also taken to the Bihar Vidyapith by Rajendra Prasad. He delivered there a highly inspiring speech. It might be recalled that a few years later J.C. Bose made a handsome donation for prohibition work in Bihar under the leadership of Rajendra Prasad. This work was done in the coalfield areas of Jharia, but could not be carried on further due to some untoward circumstances.[24]

During his tour of Bihar in 1925, he performed the opening ceremony of the Town Hall at Muzaffarpur and visited the local National School, the teachers of which were advised that they should "count no sacrifice too great if they believed that they had a message to deliver to their surroundings through their schools."[25] From Madhupur Mahatma Gandhi proceeded to Vishunpur, a village situated about 25 miles from Purnea. Mahatma Gandhi opened there a nicely built library[26] and reading room. From Vishunpur he came back to Purnea. The Purnea district supplied him with over seventeen thousand rupees, a part of which was earmarked for the Bihar Vidyapith.

Mahatma Gandhi's Bihar tour ended at Hajipur. Here he was lodged under the supervision of Dip Narayan Singh in the local school, about whom he recorded the following impression:

> "Of all the national schools in Bihar this is perhaps the best managed and the best manned, by Janakdhari Prasad, the Principal."[27]

During his Bihar tour of 1927, Mahatma Gandhi came in touch with National Schools which continued to exist in spite of tremendous odds and the general condition of which was but sad.[28] According to the report of the Bihar Vidyapith for the year 1926 there were then one College with 32 students, 15 Middle and 10 Primary Schools, affiliated to the Bihar Vidyapith as against 9, 16 and 30 respectively in the last year. The number of students reading in the High, Middle and Primary Schools were respectively 607, 983 and 483 as against 797, 1285 and 1019 of last year. The number of teachers were 67, 59 and 15 as against 69, 70 and 34. In the preceding year the High School at Bettiah had been closed for want of funds, but a Middle School was opened at Dharampur in the Purnea district in honour of Mahatma Gandhi's visit to that place. The National College at Patna had then 32 students on its roll. Lack of adequate finance was the greatest stumbling block in the path of these institutions. Another reason for their decline in number was that the Congress members, who had entered the District Boards, concerned themselves with the schools under the management of the District Boards. Mahatma Gandhi pointed out, "The school masters and the professors lacked the necessary dynamic faith in their own programme." He appealed to them to be absolutely truthful to the success of their constructive educational programme in the national schools, the curriculum of which must include spinning as a compulsory subject. He "impressed upon them the need of having an honest faith in the necessity of spinning as a vital part of a national education and of being fully qualified to teach it to their pupils." "And such a tremendous movement like hand-spinning which depends", he said, "for its success solely upon the character of the worker in it, has no chance of success, if the workers resort to camouflage."[29]

The last day of Mahatma Gandhi's Bihar tour was given to the students and professors of the Vidyapith. The Vidyapith was struggling against various impediments, chiefly financial stringency. But Rajendra Prasad and some other organisers were doing their best to maintain it by collecting funds from public subscriptions as far as possible. At Patna, some gentlemen made monthly contributions for it. Bhagwan Das had donated a plot of land, out of which accrued some income, and after sometime Gajadhar Prasad Sahu of Muzaffarpur made a gift and out of this Trust a regular income was available. To increase its efficiency and to attract people's attention towards it, it was decided by its authorities to invite some scholars of repute from outside the province. Ramdas Gaur, a learned scholar of Banaras, and some scholars from Bengal with brilliant records, were brought there. Jaichandra Vidyalankar was appointed there as Professor of History. In the second week of March 1926, Rajgopalachari addressed its annual convocation on special invitation.[30] He delivered a highly learned and thought-provoking speech on this occasion and exhorted the graduates "to cultivate the highest virtues of life to be fully ready to undergo struggles and sufferings and to affect cleanliness of heart for true and lasting deliverance of the motherland from the manifold evils from which she had been suffering."[31]

Mahatma Gradhi addressed the convocation of the Bihar Vidyapith in 1927, when Rajendra Prasad, as its Vice-Chancellor, gave away degrees to nine *snatakas.* In all the institutions the medium of instruction was Hindi, spinning was compulsory, and weaving was also taught in some of them.[32] The College was residential and the student's monthly food charges was Rs. 8 to 9 per head. Twenty-four students had till then taken their B.A. degrees and six got B.Sc. degrees. The Registrar's report contained interesting details about their post-collegiate career:

> "One of them was preparing for a diploma of the College of France, one had found an important place in business firm in Japan, one had studied dairy and cattle farming and kept a dairy of his own, two were engaged in journalism, eleven had taken up service in the national schools, one did business at Calcutta and one was engaged in Congress work."[33]

A large number of people from the city of Patna attended the convocation of the Bihar Vidyapith in the mango-grove on the back of the river Ganges near Digha. In his address, Mahatma Gandhi at the outset expressed the hope that the *snatakas* would live up to the vow they had solemnly taken that day, and "that the existence of Vidyapith would have been more than justified if it turned out one ideal student and one ideal teacher. For what was the function of these institutions ? To discover gems, no matter how few of the purest rays sever in."[34] He then spoke about negative and positive aspects of all non-cooperating institutions. These had already achieved the negative aspect by withdrawing all connection with the government. Referring to the hard lot of teachers and those who had left these institutions, he observed:

> "These troubles and sorrows are our daily lot, should be our daily lot. If observance of truth was a bed of roses, if truth cost one nothing and was all happiness and ease, there would be no beauty about it. We must adhere to truth, even if the heaven should fall. What matters it, if, by following truth, we were to lose the whole world including even India ? We shall be true votaries of truth only if we follow it to death in the conviction that under God we will get back the things we hold dear, including India. I know that a large

number of our teachers and professors are restless, a few are starving. That is true penance necessary for a proper cleansing of the national atmosphere." As regards the positive aspect of education on true national lines, which was of permanent value, he hoped that it would be fulfilled in an institution like the Vidyapith. He deprecated the "craze for more and more palatial buildings, raised out of the money of the poor, and raised for the purpose of giving an education which was denied to the poor."[35]

The Ram Krishna Vidyapith, Deoghar, was started with the chief idea of making experiment which would evolve "a new mode of education which was not precluding the assimilation of academic knowledge, would lay the main stress upon the development of character and religious spirit through a combined process of self-government and self-development of inhabitation."[36]

On account of the removal of the ban on the Congress Organisation, the Working Committee held a meeting at Wardha from 12 to 13 June 1934, and advised responsible Congress workers to expedite the re-organisation of the Congress Committees in their respective areas and engage all Congressmen in constructive activities, such as, promotion of education on national lines, spread of useful knowledge among the adult population of the villages[37] and education of girls in the province of Bihar.

The Bihar Mahila Vidyapith was founded in Darbhanga on 4 July 1934. The Vidyapith owed its inception to the energy and zeal of Pandit Rama Nand Mishra, who had led the battle for the emancipation of women throughout the province. It had secured capable guidance of the stalwart Congress leader Srikrishna Sinha.[38] Indian greatness was not likely to be achieved until Indian womanhood did not obtain a larger and a freer and fuller life; and the chief aim of the Vidyapith was to arrange for the imparting of education which would train up the daughters of Bihar into useful and cultured womanhood of happy households, "lights of the home."[39]

A National Educational Conference met at the Sadaquat Ashram, Patna, from 5 to 7 May 1937, at which Rajendra Prasad and some other Congress leaders were present and it was decided to open a number of National Schools both of the middle and secondary standards, under the control of the Vidyapith.[40] The Working Committee of the Patna Youth League held a meeting on 22 May 1937 and its President, Phulan Prasad Verma, read a paper explaining the role of socialism in national movement, and a Sub-Committee was formed to improve the organisation of the Volunteer Corps, in the town of Patna.[41]

The important Congress leaders, such as, Rajendra Prasad, Srikrishna Sinha, Anugrah Narayan Sinha, Dharnidhar, Ram Dayalu Sinha, Mathura Prasad, K.B. Sahay, P.R. Das, Badrinath Verma, Brij Bihari Chaubey, Jagat Narayan Lal, Nawal Kishore Prasad, Baldeva Sahay, Banarsi Prasad Jhunjhunwaliya and Lakshmi Narayan made a joint appeal to help the Bihar Vidyapith in the realisation of its aims and objectives. They observed, "Every country has its peculiar problems and nothing helps in their solution as effectively as a system of education based on national ideals and which takes into account the national requirements. A system of national education is, therefore, an imperative necessity for all countries; for India it is a matter of vital importance, for conditioned as the country is, the prevalent educational system is divorced from the actual life of the people and is designed to serve ends which have little to do without national requirements. National educational institutions have thus an importance which cannot be exaggerated. We, therefore, make no apology for approaching the public for help and support to the Bihar Vidyapith, Patna, which is a national educational institution in the fullest sense of the expression and has been carrying on, for over 16 years now through weal and woe, its work of producing youngmen imbued with national ideals and spirit, and fired with enthusiasm for service and sacrifice in the cause and interest of the country and its people. The Vidyapith has under it a number of schools—primary and secondary—situated in various centres of province, most of these in rural areas, and through them it carries on its work of inculcating national ideals in our boys and preparing them for national service in various fields of activities—social, econmic and political. One great aim of the institution is to bridge the gulf of, unfortunately, daily widening between the town and the country, and its course of training is so designed as to bring its alumni in direct touch with village life and condition, and thus supply the much-needed corrective to the present tendency of our educated men to look down upon, and shun the villager with the available result that rural people are being progressively devoid of light and lead, and thus of all aids to the betterment and enrichment of life. Indeed, the Vidyapith has been extremely anxious to create an active interest in rural welfare work and foster a spirit of devoted service for the all-round improvement and advancement of village life. With this end in view, it has opened a village branch, at Saho village in Darbhanga district, and has made it the centre of its post-matriculation teaching where boys will not carry on further studies under the guidance of their teacher but will also along with later study, rural problems at first hand and devote themselves to the practical work of organising, strengthening and bettering village life in all its aspects. We claim that this work of the Bihar Vidyapith and its affiliated institution has immense potentialities for national good, provided only it receives adequate pecuniary assistance as also sympathy, encouragement and cooperation. We have known that their potentialities will fructify into real benefit."[42]

Hence, during this period the people of Bihar played a commendable role in replacing the alien system of education imposed upon the nation by the National Scheme of Education. As a result, the Bihar Vidyapith was established to co-ordinate, control and guide the activities of all the national educational institutions that were springing up in different parts of Bihar. People's enthusiastic response to the Mahatma Gandhi's call to establish national schools and colleges proved this belief in his view that popular political education was of utmost importance. It was hoped that his educational plan would keep the people informed of their rights and obligations and shall prepare them for India's struggle for freedom.

References

1. Sitaramayya, B. Pattabhi, *History of the Indian National Congress*, Vol. I, p. 211.
2. Prasad, Rajendra, *Mahatma Gandhi and Bihar*, p. 43.
3. *Report of Bihar Vidyapith and its affiliated institutions*, 1921-26, by Badrinath Verma (Registrar, Bihar Vidyapith), p. 2.
4. Prasad, Rajendra, *Mahatma Gandhi and Bihar*, p. 43.
5. Ibid.
6. *Report of Bihar Vidyapith and its affiliated institutions*, p. 4.
7. *A brief sketch of the Non-Cooperation Movement*, by Rajendra Prasad, Young India, 1919-22.
8. *The Searchlight*, February 9, 1921.
9. Sitaramyya, B. Pattabhi, *History of the Indian National Congress*, Vol. I, p. 212.
10. *Report of the Bihar Vidyapith and its affiliated institutions*, pp. 4-5.
11. Ibid, pp. 6-7.
12. *The Non-Cooperation and Khilafat Movements in Bihar and Orissa*, pp. 33-34.
13. Prasad, Rajendra, *Mahatma Gandhi and Bihar*, p. 43.
14. *Report of Bihar Vidyapith*, etc., p. 12.
15. *The Searchlight*, July 19, 1922.
16. *The Non-Cooperation and Khilafat Movements in Bihar and Orissa*, p. 20.
17. Prasad, Rajendra, *Atmakatha*, p. 136.
18. Ibid.
19. Ibid, pp. 157-59.
20. *The Non-Cooperation and Khilafat Movements in Bihar and Orissa*, pp. 29-30.
21. Datta, K.K., *History of the Freedom Movement in Bihar*, Vol. I, p. 328.
22. Ibid, p. 329.
23. Ibid.
24. Prasad, Rajendra, *Atmakatha*, pp. 243-244.
25. Ibid, p. 270.
26. This library was a memorial to the deceased wife of Chaudhury Lalchand.
27. Desai, Mahadev, *Gandhiji in Indian Villages*, p. 283.
28. *Report of Bihar Vidyapith and its affiliated institutions*, (1921-26), p. 9.
29. *Young India*, 1927-28, p. 60.
30. Prasad, Rajendra, *Atmakatha*, pp. 262-264.
31. *Young India*, April 1, 1926.
32. Ibid, 1927-28, pp. 80-81.
33. *Report of Bihar Vidyapith*, etc., p. 53.

34. Ibid, p. 61.
35. Ibid, p. 63.
36. *The Searchlight*, April 15, 1931.
37. Datta, K.K., *History of the Freedom Movement in Bihar*, Vol. II, p. 230.
38. Singh, Anugrah Narayan, *Mere Sansmaran*, p. 158.
39. *The Indian Nation*, July 17, 1934.
40. Datta, K.K., *History of the Freedom Movement in Bihar*, Vol. II, p. 291.
41. *Fortnightly report of the Patna Commissioner* for the period ending May 13, 1937.
42. *The Indian Nation*, June 25, 1937.

3

Organisation of Local Arbitration Courts or Panchayats

The year 1921 witnessed events of extra-ordinary importance in Bihar as far as the establishment of popular assemblies was concerned. The Nagpur Congress gave a fillip to such events, which nonetheless related to the freedom movement in the country.[1] But in all these events Mahatma Gandhi was a source of great inspiration to the workers and delegates, who attended the Nagpur Congress from nook and corner of the country. Particularly, the delegates from Bihar returned to their respective areas of activities with the spirit and zeal of missionary and soon they absorbed themselves in the establishment of local panchayats and seva samities, whose functions were outlined in the general instructions issued to the delegates attending the Nagpur Session. The instruction included, among others, the following programmes:[2]

(i) to decide all compoundable criminal cases;

(ii) to provide primary education to the children of the village;

(iii) to look after the sanitation of the village;

(iv) to discourage the use of intoxicants;

(v) to spread swadeshi;

(vi) to raise a national fund; and

(vii) to organise a band of local volunteers to help the Sabhas in their work.

These constructive programmes made rapid progress in the different parts of Bihar in the early months of 1921. A commendable progress was made in the district of Shahabad. A meeting was held at Piro Panchayat for the trial of civil and criminal cases and this example was followed by other Panchayats, especially of the villages of Jamauli and Corhi of Rajpur Police Station; and, on their pattern, several villages in the jurisdiction of Barhara, Shahpur, Dumraon and Brahampur thanas established similar Panchayats.[3] On 13 February 1921, Swami Sivanand Brahmachari of Brahmacharya Ashram, Banaras, addressed a meeting at the Mahavir Asthan in Durgawati Police Station, in which he exhorted the audience to start Panchayats with a view of solving their problems.[4] If possible they should establish arbitration courts whose work would be either to arbitrate or take positive action for establishing a compromise between the contending parties. On his exhortion, an arbitration court was established at Doranda.[5]

The result of such activities by the workers of the Congress could be perceived in other parts of the province. The district of Saran took the lead in the formation of Panchayats. It was all due to personal attention of Rajendra Prasad and Mazharul Haque that the people took active interest, which had been justified by the government reports. One of such reports mentioned, "Panchayat had been established in a large number of villages in the following districts and were being established every day: Saran, Muzaffarpur, Champaran, Darbhanga, Patna, Gaya, Shahabad, Bhagalpur, Hazaribagh, Ranchi and Palamu."[6]

Similar attempts in the direction of arbitration courts were made by the people of the districts of Muzaffarpur and

Monghyr. In Rajkund village of the district of Muzaffarpur an arbitration court was established and Ganga Prasad Sahay, Mathura Prasad and Suraj Prasad declared themselves as 'Rashtriya Judge', 'Rashtriya Collector' and 'Magistrate' respectively.[7] In the district of Monghyr, a complainant of the village Bandhera, P.S. Gogri, filed a case before a local arbitration court presided by Doman Bhagat, Nath Sahu and Shanti Goala, promoters of Non-Cooperation Movement, in the village.[8]

A significant statement was issued by Rajendra Prasad on the working of the village panchayats in the province. According to his estimate there were several thousand panchayats, transacting cases in different villages of Bihar and it seemed that their work had been very satisfactory, because at times people resorted to social boycott with a view to enforce their decision of such panchayats.[9]

Another prominent member of the Congress, Bajrang Sahay, an inhabitant of Pachamba (Giridih district) organised the people in such a way that it soon attracted the notice of the Commissioner of Chhotanagpur, who wrote to the Inspector-General of Police, Bihar on 2 May 1921 stating, "You are perhaps aware that Non-Cooperation has probably taken a stronger hold in Giridih than anywhere else in this division. It is quite clear that they have got a very thorough organisation of volunteers and they have started panchayats and have very full-fledged system of boycott."[10]

It was also reported that the Satyagraha week brought about a tremendous change in the Bhabhua and Mohania villages, where panchayats and Seva Samities had been established in large numbers. At these two places "it was difficult to settle ponds this year except at considerably low fees as villagers were amicably settling trespass cases in the village and not taking cattle to the ponds."[11]

As far as the resolution of Bardoli Convention was concerned, many courts were established in the district of Patna. Each village in the district of Patna had a panchayat committee, which decided all matters of dispute in the village. Appeal against its decision could be made to a body, called Halka Panchayat, consisting representatives of ten to fifteen surrounding villages. From the Halka Panchayat a case might go up to the final Panchayat Board, consisting of five honest and influential men nominated by the Thana Congress Committee itself.[12] A fairly representative meeting of the Provincial Congress Committee was held at Patna on 5 January 1922 in the light of Ahmedabad resolution. In order to start Civil Disobedience, the district and Tahsil was regarded as one unit and all disputed cases were to be finally decided by the Village Panchayats.[13] According to the decision of the Bardoli Congress held on 11 and 12 February 1922, the Congress henceforth concentrated chiefly on constructive activities like vitalising of the panchayats. The Bihar Provincial Congress Committee then passed a resolution at its meeting held at Monghyr in April 1923 under the presidentship of Brajkishore Prasad stating, "It was desirable for the members of the village unions and village panchayats to mobilise the people to get their cases tried by these bodies." Before the close of the year 1923, the different political bodies likewise emphasised on constructive work at the village and district levels.[14]

The activities of the Congress workers received warm appreciation in the different parts of Bihar and for nearly four or five years the Congress engaged itself in the establishment of panchayats and arbitration courts in the distant villages of Bihar, where the people referred their disputes for amicable settlement with no grade. The leaders of the Congress visited these villages from time to time and prevailed upon them to take their cases to these local judicial bodies. Numerous such instances had come to light which exhibit the enthusiasm and belief of the people in the efficacy of the programmes of the Congress.

A very interesting example had come to light from the village of More, P.S. Mokameh, where regular sittings of the panchayats had been held under the direction of Mathura Prasad Singh, Shukhdeo Singh, Brijnandan Singh, Gaya Singh and Ram Ishwar Tiwary which decided all the petty cases of its jurisdiction. One Misharya Pasi was fined rupees five for not selling a 'ghara' of toddy to one Brijnandan Singh, who wanted it for the use of his labourers. Similarly, on the complaint of one Kantoo Pandey, the Panchayat got a culvert removed which was constructed by one Gender Dhanuk of the village over a lane. Another case of a loan of Rs. 780 taken by one Tiloo Singh, was duly considered and decided amicably. Another land dispute was between one Madan Singh of village Amta and Ram Kishun Singh of village More, which had been pending for a long time, was decided.[15] Later, on the advice of Srikant Tripathy a Congress worker of village Sitab Diara, a Committee of Panches had been started in Sitab Diara, P.S. Dhanaha, district Champaran, for the purpose of settling petty disputes.[16] As the working of the panchayat had been very successful, a meeting was held on 15 May 1929 at Kateyan, Saran in which Adya Saran Pandey appealed for the establishment of the village panchayat system in the villages of Bihar.

A case under section 147 I.P.C. was reported at Khagaria P.S. in the district of Monghyr and investigation was taken up accordingly. Some of the complainant's party were injured and were sent to the local hospital. They were told by Nemdhari Singh of Monghyr, a leading non-cooperator, that they should not produce any evidence before the Subdivisional Officer instead they should refer the case to be settled by the Panchayat of the village. He also promised to assist both the parties in settling the dispute.[17] The Shahpur Patori Congressmen had their own Subdivisional Officer, Thana Sub-Inspector, a Thana and two Subdivisional Officers, who were subsequently arrested for picketing before the administrative officials.[18] In Madhipura, the Congress people held a Swaraj Court on every Sunday in village Birah. They had appointed judge, a collector, an inspector and a daroga. Some Muhammadans of the neighbourhood also held a court, but their organisation was on less elaborate scale.[19]

Panchayats were being organised in every district of the Province. In Shahabad Panchayats had been organised in several thanas. Panchayats had been organised in fifty villages of Saran district. Panchayat organisation of Kathianrao Thana had decided 60 cases of civil disputes up to October 1930. In three days' sitting it had decided 23 cases. The panchayats in Dharhara Circle (Monghyr) in the sitting of

October 12, 1930 had decided 10 cases, which included one criminal case. The panchayat of Chaitu Circle of Samastipur was having its sitting regularly. It had decided 200 cases up to October 1930.[20] The recent Congress Programme of "Parallel Institution" seems to have attracted some notice in Shahabad. A panchayat had been started in Eklaspur.[21]

The ladies also did not lag behind. They gave greater attention to the establishment of arbitration courts and village panchayats for hearing complaints and trying cases. So far the only district which showed any indication of trying the scheme on a large scale was Shahabad, where it was proposed to group 60 villages together, each with its own panchayat, under a Head Panchayat with so-called Raja as its President with appellate powers, and a Diwan. The organisers, however, did not appear to have passed beyond the discussion stage. The Rajputs of some 60 villages of Ramgarha P.S. were making serious attempt to organise village panchayats in each of the 60 villages with a head panchayat to supervise over them. A certain man Beni Singh was to be the Raja with appellate powers and Bhirgu Singh was to set his Diwan.[22]

According to the Provincial Congress Committee's report, the village panchayats had been organised in large number. This report mentions as follows:

> "In about ten villages in the jurisdiction of thana Bihpur, panchayats have already been established and are working well. In the Santhal Parganas, in the jurisdiction of Shahebganj thana, almost all the different castes and communities have panchayats of their own through which the work of boycott is going on successfully. Ten panchayats were organised in the district of Patna and in Shahabad also the existing panchayats are working well and efforts are being made to add to their number. In Sugauli thana in the district of Champaran, the panchayats are working exceedingly well as a result of which no case goes to the law courts. Similar reports have been received of the successful organisation and working of several panchayats in the district of Saran, Monghyr and other places."[23]

The work of organising the panchayats was progressing steadily. In Barh Subdivision of the district of Patna, about 146 panchayats had already been established and they were deciding disputes and settling quarrels between people of the locality. In circle of Bihpur thana about 125 cases had so far been decided by panchayats since the beginning of the movement, but the cases had also gone to the court from this locality. In the district of Muzaffarpur, Darbhanga, Monghyr, Saran and Champaran as well, panchayats had been established and they were functioning quite effectively.[24]

The work of panchayat organisation was progressing further. In this direction, the district of Patna had much work to its credit. During the week under report about ten panchayats in Chandi thana and about 15 in Masaurhi thana had already been organised. They had begun deciding cases as well. Any one going against the decision of the panchayats had to pay a fine ranging from Rs. 10 to Rs. 25 according to the nature of the offence. In the district of Shahabad too, considerable impetus was given to the boycott work by these panchayats. In Hajipur subdivision in the district of Muzaffarpur, 50 panchayats were organised during the week under report and about 10 in the district of Purnea In the district of Darbhanga, about 10 panchayats were organised.[25]

Efforts were being made to introduce Panchayati system throughout Saran district. An arbitration court sat every Thursday at Barauli, the sitting being announced by beat of drum. Those who did not attend, were threatened with social astracism.[26] The names of the Panches of Barauli are as follows:

1. Hazari Kalwar
2. Awadh Kalwar
3. Narsing Sonar
4. Gaya Kanu
5. Ganga Barahi
6. Raiji
7. Sham Lal Singh

8. Gayadin Banwar
9. Ram Angya Kanu
10. Khub Lal Koiri
11. Hira Lal Kalwar
12. Gopal Bania
13. Raghunath Bania
14. Lakshmi Koiri
15. Sukhdeo Singh
16. Ram Bahadur.

The Congress had begun establishing caste panchayats wherever possible and preaching through it the gospel of Swadeshi, so that the people in villages might permanently decide to discard foreign cloths. This work was being entrusted tothese panchayats which would be powerful enough to enforce the observation of the decision arrived at by the panchayats. This was being done in order to infuse the spirit of swadeshi in the heart of the villagers for ever.[27]

An arbitration court and village panchayat had been established in Ranchi district. The only place where anything like a serious attempt had been made to establish a court was Bareya in Saran district. Girish Tiwary and Baban Singh were the prime movers.[28] An arbitration board was started in Darbhanga. Lakhan Prasad, Secretary, Darbhanga Arbitration Board wrote, "This Board, the Darbhanga Arbitration Board, has been started with a view to combat some of the evil efforts of litigation these days. It is a fact quite known to all, especially to the lawyers, that most of the cases which can be very well settled amicably, by the intervention of reliable and trustworthy gentlemen are brought to the law courts only for a lack of proper intervention and guidance. These very cases which can thus be settled and the differences between the parties composed amicably, entail a heavy expenditure upon the litigants. The litigant public, most of whom were but poor people, had to suffer much as the 'law delay' was proverbial. Besides this, the present day litigation weakens also the moral tone of the people which could easily be checked if the people are brought to a free and frank atmosphere of arbitration wherein much of the formalities will have no room and scope. This Board would function to give all the facilities to the people to compose their difference amicably and would decide cases which would be regarded to it in accordance with procedure laid down in the Criminal Procedure Code either privately or through the courts.

The party would be at liberty to choose any of the members of the Board as arbitrator to whom reference of this dispute should determine the matter in dispute as speedily as possible free of cost. The establishment of such an arbitration board had been a long felt want and it would, it is hoped very much, put an end to much fruitless litigation and save from ruin.

The Board, at present constituted, will consist of the following members including the office-bearers:

Presidents

1. Haribansh Shahi, Pleader, President
2. Priya Nath Mitra, Advocate
3. Ram Nihora Singh, Pleader
4. Hari Nandan Das, Pleader
5. Hemchandra Ghatak
6. Pandit Bhubneshwar Mishra
7. Lakshman Prasad

Secretary

8. Pandit Girindra Mohan Mishra, Advocate

Joint Secretaries

9. Pandit Gajadhar Mishra
10. Sone Lal Choudhury
11. Kumar Kalyani Lal
12. Harendra Kishore Choudhury

Assistant Secretaries

13. Maulvi Muhammad Safi, Bar-at-Law
14. Maulvi Muhammad Ayub
15. Maulvi Saiydul Haque
16. Upendra Nath Sinha
17. Brij Bihari Sinha
18. Sashi Nath Kanth
19. Suraj Kant Jha
20. Sukhdeo Lal Das[29]

Forty villages of Jogapatti P.S., in the district of Champaran, have, it was reported, united together and formed a panchayat of their own. Some Mussalmans of Arrah were also reported to have set up panchayat of their own with a view to checking the vicious habit of drinking and taking of other intoxicants. The number of panchayats already formed have decided disputes among the villagers.[30]

An Arbitration Board had been started at Muzaffarpur with a view to combating some of the evil effects of litigation, those days with Basanti Charan Sinha, Vakil as its President and Gaya Prasad, Vakil as Secretary. A large number of pleaders, some of whom were leading members of the Bar had volunteered their service to act on the Board and to decide cases referred to the Board without charging any fees. There were others, who for want of time had kindly offered their services only as consulting arbitrators.[31]

In April 1931, Rajendra Prasad toured several districts of the province with a view to encouraging constructive work, and much success was achieved in this respect. The only place where a Congress court was reported to be functioning effectively was Barhee, a village in the Monghyr district, had just tried its first case which was instituted in the first week of April and several cases had been filed and were pending trial. These cases appeared to be of a petty nature and no complaints had been received by the police from the parties concerned. Two were the cases of petty mischief, one referred to the catching and sale of fish from another man's ditch, and remaining one was in regard to alleged cutting of another man's crop.[32]

In addition to the Congress court established at Barhee, another court had been established at Gangasarai under Barhee Congress thana. Fee for filing complaints had been fixed at nine annas. At Barhee court both civil and criminal cases were being dealt with. The method of bringing people to justice was as follows:

If any complaint was filed before the court, the volunteers ordered the respondent to appear before the court. If he refused, he was boycotted and picketed till he was forced to appear. Then securities were demanded from both the parties in order to ensure that the decision of the court was accepted by them. Their securities were taken partly in cash and partly in handnotes. Then a full bench seated and decided the case. The decision of the court had to be obeyed; otherwise the security money was forfeited and the rebel was forced to come down by picketing and boycott. It was reported that Barhee people were thinking to establish a jail and an appellate court at this place.[33]

At Sonepur, a panchayat of people belonging to Dom, Dhobi and Chamar castes had been formed, which had decided not to use liquor or toddy in future. This had very good results and the sale of these intoxicants, therefore, had considerably gone down. Work on the above line was being started in other thanas also.[34] A panchayat court had been formed in Rohini in Deoghar P.S. under the guidance of the Congress workers. A typed letter was addressed by the Secretary of the Panchayat Court, G. Prasad, to one Permanand Prasad, liquor vendor, warning him to give up liquor business within a week or else he would be ruined. From confidential inquiries it was ascertained that about four months ago, i.e., in the month of Baisakh last, when there was a pooja at the house of Asutosh Gatwal, two barcies, viz., Thakur Bhola and Barwa were charged for outraging the modesty of girls at night, and they were fined Rs. 5 each by the panches, Kishun Prasad Misir and Lakhan Pandey. It was further learnt that on the same occasion two men, viz., Kawar

Pandey son of Harkhu Pandey and Akal Pandey son of Girija Pandey, who were charged for damaging the drum of the beaters were asked by the panches to catch hold of their ears and to sit on the ground for ten minutes for their offence.[35]

Congress panchayats were becoming common in the Sheohar thana, district Muzaffarpur. There had been two Congress panchayats only in this area—one started at Lalua in the middle of June last by Gogal Kumar, and another opened later at Sheohar National School. The attitude of Sheohar babus undoubtedly gave some encouragement to their activities, and the Sheohar Raja himself gave them some encouragement by indiscreetly agreeing to the Congress arbitration in a matter affecting his relations with his tenants. The activities of both these panchayats had, however, been very circumscribed and since the beginning of the rains, it had practically ceased altogether.[36]

The visit of Rajendra Prasad to the Shahabad area in the month of August and September 1931, was followed by "increased activities on the part of the Congress workers in regard to picketing for foreign cloth shops"[37] and greater efforts for sangathan and formation of panchayats. A Congress thana was established at Rafiganj in Gaya district which was "to decide by arbitration all cases referred to it.[38] Ram Pukar Singh was president and Jai Govind Mishra of Aurangabad was Secretary. Ram Pukar Singh decided cases.[39]

An arbitration court was established by the local Congress workers in village Kajraitha of the district of Monghyr, about 6 months ago for the purpose of deciding disputes of a civil and petty criminal cases, and that at least seven such cases had been decided in each of which a complaint fee of fourteen annas was charged. The evidence so far collected also shows that in some of the cases, the decision of the "Court" was enforced by picketing and boycott.[40]

The Town Inspector, Muzaffarpur reported that Bindheshwari Prasad Verma and Janakdhari Prasad, Congress leaders, had been selected as Panches to arbitrate in connection with a land and 'hat' disputes between the Sheohar Babu and Thakur Ramnandan Singh.[41]

An arbitration court had been established at Kuari in the Purnea district. One Latif Mian brought a civil suit against Doman Tatma, a chaukidar and Tetan Tatma, and subsequently filed his complaint also before the arbitration court. The disputes were over several plots of land. The decision of the court was signed by Ghanshyam Ray, who was one of the panches.[42]

Muneshwar Prasad, Honorary Secretary, Cooperative Health Association, visited Muzaffarpur, had prepared a scheme which he called "The Village Self-Government Scheme". Under this scheme the Panchayat Board had been organised. It decided cases of both civil and criminal nature and settled disputes. In order to enforce its order recourse may be had to the punishment prescribed in the Hindu *Shastras* which was generally social boycott and its *Prakshit*; or in the changed circumstances some other ways and means could be adopted as might be considered suitable.[43]

The Arbitration Board was appointed to arbitrate in the dispute between the management and workers of the Rohtas Industries, Dalmianagar, began its work on 4 November 1938 at Dehri. Acharya Narendradeva and Mr. Khaitan reached Dehri to decide the dispute between the management and the workers of the Rohtas Industries.[44]

The annual meeting of the villagers of Keoti P.S., Darbhanga was held on 8 November to form a panchayat of 21 members. The Panchayat Board elected Srinarayan Das, Ram Ballabh Das as president and vice-president, respectively. The Board then recognised the formation of education committee to look af'er the management of the school.[45]

An arbitration board, consisting of Shyam Nandan Singh, M.L.A., Mathura Prasad, Assistant Secretary, Bihar Pradesh Congress Committee, had been appointed to settle the Bakashta trouble existing between Harihar Prasad Sinha and the Kishan of the village Bargaon, district Shahabad. The Board failed to settle the dispute and the matter was referred to Rajendra Prasad for adjudication and award.[46]

To conclude, it can be said that the people of Bihar showed a missionary zeal in establishing local panchayats and

Seva Samities. Bihar witnessed events of extra-ordinary significance as far as the establishment of local arbitration courts was concerned. Throughout the period under review Mahatma Gandhi remained a source of inspiration to the leaders and workers of Bihar. Consequently this constructive programme made a remarkable progress in different parts of Bihar.

References

1. *1921 Movement: Reminiscence* forwarded by V.V. Giri, p. 198.
2. Datta, K.K., *History of the Freedom Movement in Bihar*, Vol. I, p. 321.
3. Ibid.
4. *The Seerchlight*, February 15, 1921.
5. Datta, K.K., *History of the Freedom Movement in Bihar*, Vol. I, p. 338.
6. *The Non-Cooperation and Khilafat Movements in Bihar and Orissa*, etc., p. 32.
7. *Extract from confidential diary of Superintendent of Police*, Muzaffarpur for the week ending March 5, 1921.
8. *Political Special File No. 69/1921, Bihar State Archives, Patna.*
9. *The Searchlight*, March 16, 1921.
10. *Letter from Commissioner of Chhotanagpur to the I.G., Police*, Bihar dated May 2, 1921.
11. Datta, K.K., *History of the Freedom Movement in Bihar*, Vol. I, p. 374.
12. *Bihar Provincial Congress Committee's report for the period* 1921.
13. Ibid., for the 1st half of January, 1922.
14. Ibid., for the first half of April, 1923.
15. *Extract from the Confidential Diary of the Superintendent of Police*, Patna, dated June 23, 1928.
16. *Extract from the Confidential Diary of the Superintendent of Police*, Champaran, dated September 23, 1928.
17. *Extract from the Confidential Diary of the Superintendent of Police*, Monghyr for the period ending May 21, 1930.

18. *Extract from the Confidential Diary of the Superintendent of Police*, Darbhanga, dated July 16, 1930.
19. *Extract from the Confidential Diary of the Superintendent of Police*, Bhagalpur for the period ending September 9, 1930.
20. *Bihar Provincial Congress Committee's report* for the week ending October 17, 1930.
21. *Extract from Mr. P.W. Murphy's fortnightly report*, D.O. No. 551/C of October 1930.
22. *Extract from D.I.G. of Police weekly report No. 1344/R, dated* October 22, 1930.
23. *The Searchlight*, November 14, 1930; *Bihar Prov. Congress Committee's report* for week ending 7-11-1930.
24. Ibid., November 21, 1930.
25. Ibid., November 28, 1930; *Weekly report of Bihar Pradesh Congress Committee* for week ending 21-11-1930.
26. *Extract from D.I.G. of Police's weekly report No. 1344/R*, dated November 11, 1930.
27. *Extract from a Special Branch Inspector's report* dated Patna, November 24, 1930.
28. *Saran District Office, D.O. No. 822/C*, dated Nov. 25, 1930.
29. *The Searchlight*, December 11, 1930.
30. Ibid., December 16, 1930.
31. Ibid., January 10, 1930.
32. *Extract from Confidential Diary of the Superintendent of Police*, Monghyr, dated May 23, 1931.
33. *Extract from Confidential Diary* for the week ending May 28, 1931.
34. *The Searchlight*, June 17, 1931.
35. *Extract from Confidential Diary of Santhal Parganas*, dated August 9, 1931.
36. *Extract from Conf. Diary of Muzaffarpur*; *D.O. No. 276-A, Sep. 1931*; *File No. 236/1931, Political Special*, Bihar State Archives, Patna.
37. *Fortnightly report of the Patna Commissioner* for the period ending September 1931.
38. *Fortnightly report of the Patna Commissioner* for the period ending September 13, 1931.
39. *Extract from the Conf. Diary of the Superintendent of Police*, Gaya dated October 2, 1931.

40. *Extract from the Conf. Diary of S.P., Monghyr*, dt. 21.12.1931.
41. Ibid., from S.P. Muzaffarpur dated 2-12-1931.
42. Ibid., from S.P. Purnea, dated 8.12 1931.
43. *The Indian Nation*, January 24, 1932.
44. Ibid., November 8, 1932.
45. Ibid., November 15, 1932.
46. Ibid., August 4, 1939.

4

Consolidation of the Congress Organisation

The year 1921 was remarkble in the history of India as it gave the country a highly organised party organisation. Before that the Congress was a constitutional party and mainly a talking body. It was Mahatma Gandhi who not ony gave a constitution and nationwide basis, but, which is more important, converted it into a revolutionary organisation.[1]

In pursuance of a clause in the resolution on Non-Co-operation passed at the Nagpur Congress, the Bihar Provincial Congress Committee issued general instruction to workers and asked them to give more attention to the work of organisation than to the delivering of speeches.[2]

The meeting of the All-India Congress Committee, held at Bezwada in the Madras Presidency on 31 March and 1 April 1921 for purely constructive work, passed a resolution asking the people to concentrate on three items:

(i) bringing the All-India Tilak Swaraj fund to one crore of rupees,

(ii) putting on the Congress register one crore of members.

(iii) introducing in the villages and the cities twenty lakhs of charkhas. All the three items were to be completed by 30 June next. The ratio fixed for Bihar was:[4]

Men	*Money*
9,42,000	9,42,000

Bihar promptly set herself to the task of fulfilling these conditions. On the commencement of the Satyagraha Week on 6 April 1921, Rajendra Prasad observed:

> "The Congress Committee had laid severe tests and we have to get through it, if we are worth anything. In this province we have to realise 10 lakhs of rupees and to enroll ten lakhs of members on the Congress register.... Let reliable volunteers visit every home and appeal to the men and women to become members of the Congress and to contribute their quota to the Tilak Swaraj Fund. In a province with a population of nearly 3 crores, 10 lakhs of rupees and members ought not to be difficult to get in the sacred Satyagraha Week. But if the people were really earnest to win swaraj, they should prove that. The Congress asked them to do three things:
>
> (1) to collect a crore of rupees on or before 30 June next. It was not a large amount for 315 millions of people. During the last war the English nation spent five crores of rupees every day. Will they hesitate to give crore of Swaraj? If they wanted Swaraj they should pay as much as they could. People should stop the small expenses, should give up smoking or eating tobacco for some time. If they gave money so spent to the Tilak Swaraj Fund, many lakhs would be collected. The Congress had asked to 10 lakhs. Patna people contributed 80,000 rupees. Would they refuse to the Congress ? The next thing the Congress wanted of them was to enlist one crore

> of members for which they had only to pay a minimum subscription of 4 annas and accept the Congress creed."[5]

The Working Committee of the All-India Congress, which met at Bombay on 23 November 1921, issued instructions for the formation of a national volunteer corps (Quami Sevak Dal). The Bihar Congress Committee at its meeting on 27 November 1921, also formed the Bihar National Volunteer Corps with its headquarter at Muzaffarpur, consisting of the following persons:[6]

1. M. Muhammad Safi
2. Dip Narayan Singh
3. Mazharul Haque
4. Arunjay Sahay Verma
5. Narayan Prasad of Chhapra

Its main duty was "to keep peace, to arrange for committees and assembly, to make arrangements at the time of processions and hartal, to serve people in the time of need, to carry out the other national work according to orders etc."[7]

The Working Committee of the Congress which met at Bardoli on 11 and 12 February 1922, directed all Congress organisations to concentrate on constructive activities like enlistment of Congress members having unflinching faith in the non-violence and collection of money for the Tilak Swaraj Fund.[8]

At a meeting of Bihar Provincial Congress Committee held at Gaya on 4 May 1922, a reception committee was formed and a number of gentlemen enrolled themselves as members. The same day donation amounting to Rs. 18,750 was promised. Work, however, had been vigorously taken up from the beginning of this month and attempt was being made to raise sufficient funds. Some parts of the Gaya district had so far been visited and promised. The various district

Congress Committees had been requested to take up work of collecting funds and enrolling members. No report has been received from any committee except that of Muzaffarpur where a few members had been enrolled and a small sum collected.[9]

On 25 January 1923, a meeting was held in the Ranchi town with P.C. Mitter as its president. He delivered a highly impressive speech exhorting the audience to devote themselves to constructive national activities. During the National Week from 6 to 13 April 1923, the local leaders made earnest efforts to collect money for the Tilak Swaraj Fund and to enlist more volunteers.[10]

On 26 February 1923, the Swaraj party of Bihar was formed at Patna with the following members:[11]

President	—Narayan Pd. of Chhapra
Secretary	—Prof. Abdul Bari, National College, Patna
Asstt. Secretaries	—Krishna Ballabh Sahay, National College, Patna Harnandan Sahay of Chhapra.

So far as enrolment of volunteers and collection for the Tilak Swaraj Fund were concerned, about 4,000 volunteers were enrolled and 41,000 rupees were collected in Bihar till the month of May 1923.[12]

At this time was started an organisation called the "Gandhi Seva Sangh" to push forward constructives activities according to the ideas of Mahatma Gandhi. Its branches were started in Bihar, but no centre was established in Bihar for its work. After a few years an attempt was made in this direction at village Mairva in Saran district, but it did not prove fruitful.[13]

Bihar Provincial Conciliatory Board requested its subordinate committee throughout Bihar to enroll one lakh Congress members by 18 March 1924.[14]

Mahatma Gandhi's Bihar trip this time began with his attending the Bihar Provincial Conference at Purulia in September 1925. At Bishunpur the people presented a good purse for the Deshbandhu Memorial Fund. Mahatma Gandhi's Bihar tour ended at Hajipur, where a purse of about Rs. 5,000 was presented to him. The total collection throughout his Bihar tour then amounted to Rs. 1,50,000. A portion of it was added to the capital of the All-India Spinners' Association.[15]

Mahatma Gandhi's second Bihar tour in this period began from January 1927. At Mairva he addressed a mammoth meeting of over 30,000 people. This meeting was "at once a model of orderliness and the biggest" that Mahatma Gandhi had addressed this time in Bihar. "Empty your pocket for the poor" was his short message. There was a generous response to it, the total of the villagers' contributions being worth Rs. 1,000 in piles of coins, which had to be carried by three men." At Gaya a purse collection may well have been better if it had been better organised." The largest collection during the Bihar tour was made on 18 January when Rs. 6,500 were received from Dalsingsarai, Samastipur and Darbhanga.[16]

The Congress at its Calcutta session of 29 December 1928 also passed a resolution outlining future programme of constructive work for Congressmen. Such works were strengthening of the Congress organisation by enlisting members. To give effect to this resolution, the Bihar Provincial Congress Committee immediately after the Calcutta Session had been over, addressed all the district Congress Committees, among other matters, on the need for enrolling a large number of Congress members and strengthening the Congress organisation where these already existed and starting new ones, where they did not. This matter was not taken up seriously except by a very few of the district Congress Committees. But after the penal resolution[17] of the All-India Congress Committee, the other district Congress Committees also became active. The penal resolution is as follows:

"Provincial Congress Committee shall have—

(i) not less than one-quarter per cent of the total population of their province as original members;

(ii) not less than fifty per cent of the district in the Provincial Congress Committee.

District and Tahsil organisation shall have not less than one-quarter per cent of the population as original members. In the case of the district not less than fifty per cent of the Tahsil must be represented in it and in the case of the Tahsil not less than ten per cent of the village within the Tahsil should be represented.

A village organisation shall have not less than one per cent of the population as original members....

In computing the quota of each province or district, the Indian states and the agency corresponding to non-regulation tracts need not be taken into account.

No provincial organisation will be recognised unless it satisfies the following tests by August 31, 1929."

Passed its resolution at Bombay meetings on 24 and 25 May 1929, all the districts began to make strenuous efforts to fulfil the quota of membership on the date fixed by the All-India Congress Committee (31 August). The result was that Bihar was able to enrol above 80,000 members by that time whereas its quota was for 72,558 members. By the end of 1929, there were 90,525 Congress members in this province.[18]

The organised districts of this province had their subdivisional or thana committees, from which they elected representatives to their district. The district of Champaran was first in the matter of organisation as it had village committees also in some of the thanas. The second place was that of Darbhanga, which would enrol about double its quota in a fortnight only. Some of the other districts tried to organise village committees but with no success.[19]

During the Mahatma Gandhi's historic march to Dandi, the zeal of patriotism was remarkable in Bihar. Independence Day was celebrated here with great solemnity. Congress members were being enrolled in large number.[20] Figures of the members enrolled till about the middle of February 1930 was as follows:

Sl. No.	District	No. of Members
1.	Champaran	1568
2.	Chhapra	6252
3.	Darbhanga	350
4.	Bhagalpur	770
5.	Monghyr	650
6.	Purnea	200
7.	Santhal Parganas	150
8.	Patna (Rural)	1910
9.	Gaya	400
10.	Shahabad	700
11.	Hazaribagh	1400
12.	Ranchi	1000
13.	Manbhum	379
14.	Patna City	800

The Bihar Provincial Congress Committee met at Sadaquat Ashram, Patna, under the presidentship of Rajendra Prasad on 30 March 1930 to devise ways and means for the implementation of the resolution passed in the Congress Committee held at Ahmedabad in March 1930. It proposed to enrol at least fifty thousand volunteers in the province. Sixty-one members of the Provincial Congress Committee signed the volunteer pledge. Among those were:

1. Rajendra Prasad
2. Narayan Pd. Sinha
3. Jaleshwar Prasad
4. Mathura Prasad
5. Ram Bilash Sharma.[21]

All the Congress workers of the Purnea district had been directed to enlist as many as 4,000 Congress members throughout the district. The work had been started in right earnest.[22]

A meeting of the Working Committee of the Gaya District Congress Committee took place at Jamhore on 3 May 1931 under the presidentship of Gauri Shankar Sharan Sinha. It was resolved that up to 31 May each sub-division should complete the quota of membership positively.[23]

The Working Committee of Aurangabad Sub-divisional Congress Committee met at Jamhore. Badri Narayan Sinha was in the chair. It was resolved that each thana of the sub-division should complete the quota of membership by 31 May.[24]

On 4 May 1931, at Kajur, a meeting was held under the presidentship of Chandradeo Narayan Sinha, who appealed the audience to enrol themselves as Congress members.[25]

A meeting of the Muzaffarpur District Congress Committee was held on 3 May under the presidentship of Bideshwari Prasad Verma. The Committee further resolved to enrol allotted Congress members before the 31st May. Finally it adopted the following resolution regarding Hindustani Seva Dal: "That inasmuch as it had been proved by experience that it was necessary to have a band of trained disciplined volunteers, this Committee resolves to help the Hindustani Seva Dal as far as may be possible in organising volunteers in this district." A tour programme was also arranged for the entire district for explaining the Congress resolution and enrolling the Congress members.[26]

A big public meeting was held at Mangles Tank, Patna City. Rajendra Prasad and Jagat Narayan Lal addressed the audience. Rajendra Prasad, who was not keeping well, made short speech on the present Congress programme. He emphasised on strengthening the organisation of the Congress and said that it must be very strong and efficient. He enquired whether every Mohalla of the City had a Mohalla Committee and a Mohalla Panchayat. If it had not already been done, the organisation was haphazard. According to the decision of the Provincial Congress Committee, elections must be over by 15 June. The real purpose of the election was that there should be as large number of members as possible, so that it might be proved that the Congress was really a representative body. Every Congress worker must select a certain mohalla and visit every house to enlist members. He must explain to the people fully the implication of the Congress membership form. They became firm supporters of the Congress. During the last Satyagraha campaign many people did join who were not even Congress members.[27]

Satya Narayan Sinha, accompanied by Jay Narayan Jha visited village Bela, district Samastipur, where a largely attended meeting was held. People were asked to take up the constructive programme in right earnest and enrol in large number as members of the Congress.[28]

The first meeting of the newly constituted Working Committee of the Muzaffarpur Town Congress Committee was held in the Tilak Maidan under the presidentship of Sarju Prasad, where it was decided to grant Rs. 20 to the Hindustani Seva Dal for meeting the expenses of the officers' training camp, which was going to be started at Muzaffarpur from 15 June 1931.[29]

Ekma Thana Congress Committee in the district of Chhapra completed its quota, which was 618 members, and had enrolled even more than its quota. Banipur thana also completed her quota required.[30]

Intensive campaign for enlisting Congress members was going on in the Madhubani district. Atul Chandra Ghosh, Sashdhar Ganguli, Jimut Bhushan Das Gupta, Bimalendu Das Gupta and others were touring in different parts of the district.[31]

Pandit Bedvertaji accompanied by Pandit Girish Tiwary, Secretary, Chhapra District Congress Committee, laid stress on enrolling Congress members and to complete quota soon at Mirganj, Bhore, Raghunathpur and Darauli.[32]

Satya Narayan Sinha accompanied by Jadunandan Sahay, went to Singhia Thana of Samastipur district for Congress work. Ram Charan Sinha joined them one day later. In the evening of 19 June 1931, public meeting attended by a very large number of people, was held at Sumbha Deodhi where an address neatly printed on khadi and a purse containing Rs. 302 were presented to Satya Narayan Sinha, the first dictator of the district.[33]

The Bettiah Sub-divisional Congress Committee had so far (till last week) enrolled 1157 Congress members and formed 55 Congress Ashrams.[34]

At Ranchi, in a Conference, Mahatma Gandhi agreed to recommend to the All-India Congress Committee that the Swaraj Party be authorised to function as the parliamentary party of the Congress enjoying autonomy, subject to formulation of the national demand as formulated by the Congress. In pursuance of the Congress creed and adoption of repeal of repressive laws and release of political prisoners were a part of the party programme. The Congress Working Committee would keep a watch over the Swaraj Party's activities so that, while enjoying autonomy, it did not violate the Congress creed.[35]

The party would stand for an equitable adjustment between capitalist and labour, landlord and tenants and work for the relief of agricultural indebtedness, promote inter-communal unity, work for removal of untouchability and the promotion of the Congress constructive programme.[36]

In accordance with the circular passed by the Secretary, Bihar Provincial Congress Committee, a meeting of the workers of the Bihar Province was called at the residence of Seth Jamna Lal Bajaj. Srikrishna Singh, Member of the Parliamentary Board, was in the chair. Though the meeting was formal one, about sixty members were present. After three hours' long discussion the workers chalked out a plan for carrying on Congress work in different districts of the province. The workers were directed to enroll one per cent of the total population in their areas and complete the organisation of all committees in the district by the end of August.[37]

A meeting of the Congress workers of Hajipur Sub-division was held near the old Gandhi Ashram, which was under the control of government, with Kishori Prasanna Sinha as its President. Resolution of the Congress Working Committee suspending Civil Disobedience Movement and calling upon Congressmen to re-organise the Congress

Committees, were explained. The following gentlemen were deputed with receipt books to organise and enroll members in different thanas mentioned against their names:[38]

Lalit Singh and Akshabat Singh	Mahua thana
Swami Atmanand	Patepur thana
Pandit Madan Jha	Mahnar thana
Jagannath Prasad	Lalganj thana
Phekan Singh and Sukhdeo Lal	Raghopur thana.

Just after the meeting of the All-India Congress Committee was held and decided to withdraw the Civil Disobedience Movement for the first time in the province and decided to start the organisation work, since then a number of meetings had met and decided to take up the work in full swing. The enrolment of members was going on.[39]

The District Congress Committee of Muzaffarpur decided to start the work of enrolment of members of the Congress.[40]

A largely attended meeting of the Hazaribagh District Congress Committee was held on 3 July 1934. The prominent members of the Committee, who attended the meeting undertook to enrol a certain number of Congress members totalling in all 1,000. Two paid workers were appointed to undertake the enrolment of members. In order to organise the whole district and push on the enrolment work, it was arranged that Ram Narayan Singh and Saraswati Devi should tour to whole district.[41]

The Patna District Congress Committee was busy enrolling four annas members. Till the second week of July 1934. 2106 members had been enrolled from different places as follows:[42]

Barh Sub-division	567
Bihar Sub-division	475
Patna Sadar Sub-division	272
Danapur Sub-division	792

Kishori Prasanna Singh, with the help of other Congress workers, was able to re-organise Congress in Hajipur Sub-division. The enrolment of Congress members was just over and they were then in position to complete figures of this Sub-division, which are as follows:[43]

Patepur Thana	91
Mahnar Thana	180
Raghopur Thana	103
Hajipur Thana	225
Mahua Thana	234
Lalganj Thana	467

During the year 1935-36, there were all throughout active preparations on the part of the Congress as also on that of others for election. According to the government statement the total number of persons enrolled by Congress was about 78,000 and of all the provinces in India, Bihar enrolled the largest number of members.[44]

Rajendra Prasad, President, All-India Congress Committee, addressed a largely attended meeting at the Kadamkuan Congress Maidan on 19 February 1936. Speaking of the task before the Congress and its programme, Rajendra Prasad said that the Congress should divert its energy towards constructive programme now going forward, which was the only programme before the Congress. He also said that it would be wrong to think that the Congress had receded from its original ideals of Swaraj. The change in the method and programme of the Congress showed that it was a live organisation, for only such organisations changed their ideals according to the need of the time.[45]

An ordinary meeting of the Saran District Congress Committee was held at Maharajganj under the presidentship of Mahamaya Prasad Sinha. A resolution deciding to enrol about 2,000 members for the Congress from this district as well urging prominent Congress workers including the non-official Congress workers to make a tour of the whole district was also passed.[46]

A conference of the Thana Congress Committee of Sandesh Thana in the district of Shahabad was held on 25 April 1937, under the presidentship of Harnandan Singh, Advocate, M.L.A. of the Provincial Thana Congress, which was constituted with Subhuji as president and Ram Bilash Sah as secretary. It was resolved to enrol at least 3,000 Congress members by the end of June and exhorted the people to increase the strength of the Congress by organising Congress Committees and enrolling members.[47]

A meeting of the working committee of the Saran District Congress Committee was held at Mashrakh on 1 May 1937. Mahamaya Prasad Sinha was President. A Provincial Reception Committee for the 20th Bihar Provincial Political Conference, consisting of 15 members with Prabhunath Singh, was formed. Membership fee for the reception committee was fixed at Rs. 2 and it was decided to raise Rs. 5,000 by enrolment of members.[48]

A meeting of the Bakhtiarpur Thana Congress Committee was held at Gonawan on 13 May 1937 under the presidentship of Shilbhadrayaji, M.L.A. It was decided to enrol 1,200 members within a month and workers were allotted a portion according to their capacity.[49]

An informal meeting of some of the members of the Town Congress Committee, Bhagalpur was held. Prominent amongst those present were Upendra Nath Mukherjee, M.L.A., Kailash Bihari Lal, Ganga Prasad, Baldeva Sahai, Maulvi Sarif and others. It was decided to enrol at least 130 members from each of the nine wards of the town and vigorous steps be taken to organise the Town Congress Committee.[50]

A meeting of the Patna District Congress Committee was held under the presidentship of Ganga Sharan Sinha in the Committee Room of the Patna District Congress Office. It decided to devote the days from 3 June to 30 June 1937, exclusively for enrolment of members. Every member was requested to participate and enrol members and submit reports to the District Congress Committee. It was further decided that every member should contribute Rs. 5 from his own pocket and collect and remit the same by June 30 to meet the expenses of the District Congress Committee.[51]

The district of Patna also took the work of enrolling members earnestly. Following was the number of members enrolled till the first week of June 1937 in the different Thanas of the District of Patna:[52]

Punpun	54
Behar	152
Ekanger Sarai	190
Islampur	80
Naubatpur	68
Chandi	40
Dinapur	269
Bakhtiarpur	115
Barh	320
Masaurhi	90
Hilsa	130
Asthawan	20
Bikram	300

Through Ishwari Prasad 110; through Kailash Pati Singh 10; and through Ram Sewak Singh 61; total 1915.

The Jamshedpur Congress Committee was engaged in enrolling Congress members. Mohammadans were too enlisting themselves as members. A public meeting was held in Marwari Thakurwari where Kumar K.P. Singh exhorted the audience to enrol themselves as Congress members and engage themselves in Congress work.[53]

The following circular regarding the membership had been issued by the Secretary, Patna Town Congress Committee:

The 30th September 1937 was the last date in the current year for the enrolment of Congress members. All the applications for membership together with the necessary fees as well as the blank forms must be submitted by 10 P.M. on 3 October 1937.[54]

The work of enrolling Congress members was proceeding very briskly throughout Bettiah Sub-division. The programme had completely occupied by the local Congress workers.[55]

In Hajipur Sub-division a remarkable progress was made. Over 18,000 members were enrolled till 30 September 1937.[56]

From reports received so far at the headquarters of the Bihar Provincial Congress Committee, it was learnt that about 40 thousand Congress members were enrolled in the district of Darbhanga, 34 thousand in Purnea, 4 thousand in Singhbhum as against 530 of last year; 5,954 in Patna town as against 1,012 of last year and 1,378 in Barahia thana.[57]

The Secretary, Motihari District Congress Committee, announced that this year 32,775 members had enrolled in the district of Champaran.[58]

The following was the list of primary membership received by the Bihar Provincial Congress Committee when dispatched to All-India Congress Committee so far:

Darbhanga	70,500
Muzaffarpur	61,716
Shahabad	48,426
Champaran	36,772
Patna Town	5,346
Singhbhum	4,620
Hazaribagh	4,355
Santhal Parganas	3,664
Monghyr	36,064
Bhagalpur	29,653
Patna District	29,290
Gaya	26,358
Palamau	3,272
Ranchi	2,857
Manbhum	2,418
Grand Total	4,48,384

Out of 4,48,384, twenty-five thousand were Muslims.[59]

A mammoth public meeting attended by two thousand, both Hindus and Muslims, was held in the evening of 5 November 1937 at Nuruddinpur (my own village), P.S. Fatwa in the district of Patna, under the presidentship of Muhammad Khalil Ahmad in a well decorated shamiyana. Pandit Sheel Bhadrayajee, M.L.A., addressed the gathering for more than an hour in which he explained to the audience the programme of the present Bihar Ministry and exhorted the peasants to join the Congress and not to do any illegal work.[60]

The President, Muhammad Khalil, also spoke in which he appealed both the Hindus and Muslims to join the Congress in large numbers.[61]

The Bihar Provincial Rajwar Conference commenced here under the presidentship of Bathu Ram. Jaglal Chaudhary, Shyam Narayan Singh, M.L.A., Jagjivan Ram also attended the meeting. The distinguished visitors exhorted Rajwar to give up drinking and to enrol themselves as Congress members.[62]

A mass meeting was held at Karaiya, four miles off from Dumka, attended mostly by Santhals. Pandit Biswanath Upadhyaya, A.M.S., the present Secretary of Dumka Congress Committee, delivered a nice speech appealing the masses to give up the evil habit of drinking. Being impressed by his speech, a good number of persons enrolled themselves as Congress members.[63]

Bettiah Subdivisional Harijan Conference was held at Madhubani with Jamuna Ram in chair. Bal Govind Bhagat, M.L.A. delivered a very nice speech. He laid stress on organisation and asked the audience to strengthen the Congress by becoming its member in large number.[64]

Pandit Sudhi Nath Jha 'Kairab', M.L.A. incharge of the Santhal Parganas District Congress Committee made an extensive tour throughout the Jamtara Subdivision. He held several meetings in both the Subdivisions where a large number of persons were enrolled as Congress members. At Garia, a meeting was held which was attended by 3,000 villagers. It is reported that the number of Congress members in the district would exceed 25,000 this year while the figure of last year was only 3,000. Credit went to the Executive of Dumka and Godda Thana Congress Committee for the increase in the number of Congress members. It was reported that the Deoghar Thana Congress Committee could not do well this year.[65]

Jagat Narayan Lal, addressing the Santhal Conference at Chirki, explained the Congress programme and measures taken by the Congress ministry. He was loudly cheered when he said that real swaraj had yet to be achieved and all the Santhals should strengthen the Congress and be ready to make sacrifice when called upon to do so.[66]

It was expected that the number of 4-annas Congress members in Bhagalpur district would come to 45,000 this year.[67]

Before a large gathering consisting of leading citizens and prominent workers of the Madhubani Subdivision and Municipal Commissioner Harihar Prasad Mahaseth requested the audience to join the Congress. He assured the audience that he would always keep fresh in mind the basic Congress principles, truth and non-violence. Prominent among those present were Chit Nath Jha, Lakshmi Nath Mishra, Anirudh Sinha, Arjun Sinha, Rajendra Narayan Chaudhary, Sital Sinha, Raj Kishore Prasad, Sushit Kumar Rai and Jagdish Jha.[68]

The Bihar Provincial Congress Committee received the following figures of primary members enlisted in the course of the year 1938 from 17 districts (including the Patna District Congress Committee) in the province. Muzaffarpur topped the list. The figures of Musalman members was not exactly known then but from the report available, each district registered a very large number of Muslim members.

District	*Members enrolled*
Muzaffarpur	91,000
Bhagalpur	51,125
Darbhanga	50,735
Purnea	44,892
Monghyr	43,651

Shahabad	41,250
Patna D.G.C.	39,439
Champaran	34,288
Saran	32,974
Singhbhum	30,351
Gaya	28,899
Santhal Parganas	24,200
Hazaribagh	14,775
Palamau	12,171
Ranchi	11,955
Manbhum	7,976
Patna Town Cong. Comm.	3,997
Total	5,62,678[69]

Manzur Ahsan Ejazi, Secretary, Muzaffarpur District Congress Committee, in course of the statement to the Indian Nation, congratulated all office-bearers for doing a great job. He added that the number of members had distinctly increased by 50% over the total enrolment last year. He further congratulated the Musalmans in general, who had joined the Congress in large numbers this year despite the vigorous propaganda launched by the Muslim League. The total number of Muslim members of the Congress came to 4,000 (four times that of the figure of the last year). He added that there had been two great questions amongst the Congress Muslims of Muzaffarpur by the enrolment of Mohammad Jafar, Bar-at-Law, and Syed Ejaz Husain Jafery, Ph.D.[70]

Syed Mohammad, Secretary of Daudnagar Sifton High School, a prominent man of Gaya district, resigned from Muslim League and joined Congress.[71]

Enquiry at the Headquarters of the Bihar Congress Committee showed that in the year 1939, the number of Congress members en[illegible]ed would be much less than that achieved last year. Though the last date for enrolment was

15 September 1939, yet there was no likelihood that this short time would be utilised to speed up the work and make up the deficiency.[72]

The Purnea District Congress Committee had enlisted 23,433 primary Congress members in 1939. It was expected that the total number of primary members would exceed 25,000 this year.

The following was the quota for members from each of the three sub-divisions of this district: Araria 7,131; Kishanganj 4,471; Sadar 11,831. Selection of volunteer for Ramgarha Congress was made for two days.[73]

The Congress workers of all shades of opinion of Katra Thana in Muzaffarpur district decided to enrol the Congress volunteers and to keep them engaged in constructive works.[74]

Ram Narayan Singh, M.L.A. (Central) accompanied by Sukhlal Singh, the first non-official Chairman of the District Board, Hazaribagh, addressed a public meeting held in the Giridih Municipal Compound. He appealed the audience to help in enrolment of Congress members and both made strong plea for sinking all communal differences.[75]

A careful perusal of the above facts proves that Bihar promptly set herself to the task of consolidating the Congress Organisation. Bihar witnessed profound awakening since the Nagpur Congress. Popular enthusiasm for the cause of nationalism was daily rising high and recruitment of volunteers was being made in large numbers. People were contributing liberally to the Tilak Swaraj Fund. Mahatma Gandhi's Bihar tours gave additional impetus to the consolidation work which had the effect of rousing the whole Province into action. The work of consolidation generated passionate zeal among the masses and due to this Bihar "stood the test of the time and government repression."

References

1. Dodwell, H.H., *The Cambridge History of India*, Vol. VI, p. 774.
2. Dutta, K.K., *History of the Freedom Movement in Bihar*, Vol. I, p. 326.

3. Bamford, P.C., *History of the Non-Cooperation and Khilafat Movement*, p. 27.
4. Datta, K.K., *History of the Freedom Movement in Bihar*, Vol. I, p. 369.
5. *The Searchlight*, April 6, 1921.
6. Datta, K.K., *History of the Freedom Movement in Bihar*, Vol. I, vide Appendix XV.
7. Ibid., *History of the Freedom Movement in Bihar*, Vol. I, p. 402.
8. Ibid., p. 416.
9. *The Searchlight*, July 19, 1922.
10. Datta, K.K., *History of the Freedom Movement in Bihar*, Vol. I, pp. 444-45.
11. *The Non-Cooperation and Khilafat Movement in Bihar and Orissa*, p. 112.
12. *The Searchlight*, June 6, 1923.
13. Prasad, Rajendra, *Atmakatha*, p. 213.
14. *The Searchlight*, March 7, 1924.
15. Desai, Mahadev, *Gandhiji in Indian Villages*, pp. 238-280.
16. *Young India*, 1927-28, p. 77.
17. Datta, K.K., *History of the Freedom Movement in Bihar*, Vol. II, p. 11.
18. *Annual report of the Congress Secretary for 1929 : Bihar Provincial Congress Committee Annual Report*, 1928-29.
19. Datta, K.K., *History of the Freedom Movement in Bihar*, Vol. II, p. 12.
20. *The Searchlight*, February 14, 1930.
21. Ibid., April 2, 1930.
22. Ibid., April 12, 1931.
23. Ibid., May 5, 1931.
24. Ibid., May 10, 1931.
25. Ibid.
26. Ibid.
27. Ibid., June 3, 1931.
28. Ibid., June 5, 1931.
29. Ibid., June 6, 1931.
30. Ibid.
31. Ibid., June 18, 1931.
32. Ibid., June 26, 1931.

33. Ibid.
34. Ibid., June 27, 1931.
35. *The Indian Nation*, May 4, 1934.
36. Ibid.
37. Ibid., June 13, 1934.
38. Ibid., June 20, 1934.
39. Ibid., June 27, 1934.
40. Ibid., June 29, 1934.
41. Ibid., July 8, 1934.
42. Ibid., July 18, 1934.
43. Ibid., August 23, 1934.
44. *The Non-Cooperation and Khilafat Movement in Bihar and Orissa* in 1935-36, p. 7.
45. *The Indian Nation*, February 10, 1936.
46. Ibid., March 20, 1936.
47. Ibid., April 21, 1937.
48. Ibid., May 7, 1937.
49. Ibid., May 19, 1937.
50. Ibid., May 21, 1937.
51. Ibid., June 9, 1937.
52. Ibid.
53. Ibid , June 23, 1937.
54. Ibid., October 1, 1937.
55. Ibid., October 5, 1937.
56. Ibid., October 14, 1937.
57. Ibid., October 21, 1937.
58. Ibid., November 2, 1937.
59. Ibid.
60. Ibid., November 9, 1937.
61. Ibid.
62. Ibid., April 13, 1938.
63. Ibid., May 13, 1938.
64. Ibid., October 26, 1938.
65. Ibid.
66. Ibid., October 29, 1938.
67. Ibid., November 13, 1938.

68. Ibid., November 16, 1938.
69. Ibid., December 2, 1938.
70. Ibid., December 11, 1938.
71. Ibid., December 15, 1938.
72. Ibid., August 26, 1939.
73. Ibid., October 31, 1939.
74. Ibid., November 9, 1939.
75. Ibid., November 19, 1939.

5

Promotion of Communal Harmony

In pursuance of a clause in the resolution on Non-Cooperation passed at the Nagpur Congress, the Bihar Provincial Congress Committee issued a general instruction to the workers, "Efforts should be made to strengthen Hindu-Muslim unity, and all cases of friction between the two communities must be removed."[1]

During the days of Satyagraha the most heartening phenomenon was the fraternisation of the Hindus and the Muslims. The Hindus forgot their taboos about food and drink and accepted what a Muslim offered. The Muslims invited Hindu leaders to their mosques to give addresses. Swami Shradha Nand preached in the great mosque of Delhi, Jama Masjid. Gandiji and Sarojini Naidu spoke in a mosque at Bombay. Muslims identified themselves with the Hindus in the Hartals and Satyagraha. Gandhi and Muhammad Ali jointly directed the nationalist movement.[2]

Gandhiji said once on Khilafat question, "It is just my sense of moral responsibility which had made me take up the Khilafat question and to identify myself entirely with the Muhammadans. It is perfectly true that I am assisting in countenancing the unions between Hindus and Muslims.[3]

Rajendra Prasad made a speech a: Bhabhua on 27 February 1921 asking the audience "to foster the unity between Hindus and Muhammadans." "It so happens," he said, "that both Hindus and Musalmans, Hindus and Hindus and Muhammadans and Muhammadans fight amongst themselves, a state of feeling which should be driven out of the mind, because if a foreigner comes and sees it he will hold a very low opinion of the people. You Hindus and Muhammadans live in one country, eat the produce of the same soil, go back to the same earth after death, then why should not unite yourselves ?"[4]

Rajendra Prasad having received two private letters from Gandhiji, both purporting to a complaint on the cow killing in Bihar and Orissa, called a joint Hindu-Muslim conference in the National College on 29.5.1921 to devise means to settle the differences and to inform Gandhiji accordingly.[5]

In opening the meeting, Rajendra Prasad said that Gandhiji writes that the Muslim should on no account be compelled to give up cow killing, but should be requested to give it up by and by for the betterment of India. Volunteers should be warned not to compel anyone to abstain from drinking or do anything against the principles of non-cooperation, but at the same time they should not refrain from requesting people to do the right thing. When the present demands and aims of the Hindus and Muslims were one and the same they should try not to wound the feeling of each other. Rajendra Prasad asked the gentlemen present to discuss and settle the matter and the means to be adopted for settling the Hindu-Muslim feeling."[6]

Amongst the prominent men present were:

1. Dip Narayan Singh — Bhagalpur
2. Rajendra Prasad — Patna
3. Brij Kishore Prasad — Darbhanga
4. Mohammad Shafi — Muzaffarpur
5. Gorakh Prasad — Motihari
6. Mohammad Zubair — Monghyr
7. Mohammad Mahfooz Alam — Shahabad

8.	Mohammad Zakaria Hashmi	Saran
9.	B.K.P.S. Sinha	Gaya
10.	Qazi Ahmd Husain	Gaya
11.	Hari Prasad	Gaya
12.	Mohammad Sajjad	Gaya.[7]

In the discussion it was considered that the ehief cause of present Hindu-Muslim feeling was that the government had smuggled in some of her own men into the Seva Samities, who were fomenting the feeling. Hence attempts should be made to warn Seva Samiti members to be non-violent in their action and also to dismiss those from the Seva Samities who were disobeying the order to be non-violent.[8]

In the end a Provincial Board was formed of the following members to carry out the propaganda detailed below:

1.	Dip Narayan Singh	Bhagalpur
2.	Rajendra Prasad	Patna
3.	Dr. Mahmood	Patna
4.	Shah Nurul Hasan	Phulwarisharif, Patna
5.	Hafiz Zahid Saheb	—do—
6.	Brij Kishore Prasad	Darbhanga
7.	K.P.S. Sinha	Gaya
8.	Mohammad Shafi	Muzaffarpur
9.	Mohammad Zubair	Monghyr.

Neither a President nor a Secretary was selected, but Dip Narayan Singh was to work as President and Rajendra Prasad as Secretary of the above-mentioned Provincial Board.[9]

The following suggestions were passed by the Board to be put in the effect at once:

"1. That notices be published and circulated in Hindi and Urdu by responsible and selected volunteers in only those places which are affected by the cow killing questions; the notices to contain the wishes and orders of Gandhiji on the subject and an appeal from the Provincial Board of Bihar & Orissa.

2. That 5 Pandits and 5 Maulvis be selected by the district affected to go to the affected areas, preach non-violence, explain the situation from the political and religious points of view on cow killing, and request both the sects not to compel each other to do a thing or not to do a thing against one's free will. Muslims should persuade Muslims not to kill cows and Hindus should persuade Hindus not to interfere but to appeal to them and not persist, if unheard. Names were not selected. Any particular district is empowered to mobilise or invite any person of influence in that district, e.g., Abul Kalam Azad should be among those."[10]

The efforts made to settle the differences between the two communities through the 'Anti Kine Killing Agitation' did not seem to have met with much success. A communication sent from Monghyr to the Secretary of the Central Khilafat Committee, Bombay, states as follows:

> "The condition of Muslims here is very bad. Hindus do not allow Musalmans the use of beef or any kind of meat in the village of this district. The Hindus who inhabit the villages were called 'Babhna' and their religious belief is that it is the Muhammadans who will destroy the Hindus and therefore they are bent upon doing mischief. Now some Hindus prepare arms in the villages and they sell them to Hindus alone."[11]

Whatever might be the plea of the Government, Mahatma Gandhi and his followers were eager to maintain peace. To prevent any untoward incident during the approaching Bakr-Id, and to strengthen Hindu-Muslim unity,

Mahatma Gandhi undertook a tour of seven days, accompanied by Maulana Muhammad Ali, Abdul Qadir Sobhani, Seth Jamna Lal Bajaj and some others. The party visited Buxar, Dumraon, Koath, Bikramganj and Sasaram in the Shahabad district; Aurangabad, Sherghati, Gaya and Nawada in the Gaya district and Biharsharif in the Patna district.[12] The meeting at Biharsharif was attended by a large number of weavers and Mahatma Gandhi delivered a soul-stirring speech on this occasion. The Biharsharif Municipality presented an address of honour and welcome to Mahatma Gandhi and at Buxar too Satya Narayan Lal presented him a similar address on behalf of the local Municipality, of which he was the Vice-Chairman.[13]

Meeting at Delhi on 4 and 5 November 1921, the All-India Congress Committee authorised every province its own responsibility to undertake Civil Disobedience including non-payment of taxes. The conditions were many but one of them was that in the event of individual civil disobedience, the individual "must be a believer in Hindu-Muslim unity and unity among all the communities professing different religions in India as an article of faith, must believe in Non-violence as absolutely essential for the redress of the Khilafat and the Punjab wrongs and the attainment of Swaraj."[14]

Soon after returning from Ahmedabad, the prominent Bihar delegates began to consider how best they could carry out latest instructions of the Congress. A fairly representative meeting of the Provincial Congress Committee was held on 5 January 1922 to discuss the future plan of action in the light of the Ahmedabad resolutions. The instructions were issued to the District Congress Committees. The instructions related to communal harmony were as follows:

> "The union among Hindus, Muslims and other communities should be strengthened so that men of all castes and creeds be of one heart."[15]

The Working Committee of the All-India Congress met at Bardoli on 11 and 12 February 1922 and passed a resolution suspending mass civil disobedience movement and directed the organisation to "concentrate on constructive activities."[16]

After May 1923, Gandhi Seva Sangh was organised to push forward the constructive activities. Mahatma Gandhi particularly pleaded for communal harmony which took the form of inculcating in all hearts and minds love for Hindu-Muslim unity, going so far as to support even the Khilafat Movement in the hope of bringing the Muslims on his side. Before the close of the year 1923, the different political bodies in Bihar discussed some significant matters. The Bihar Provincial Conference met at Motihari on 31 October and 1 November 1923, under the presidentship of Dharindhar of Darbhanga. Resolutions were passed reaffirming faith in Mahatma Gandhi's Non-violent, Non-Cooperation and emphasizing on constructive works. This was followed by the Khilafat Conference over which Maulana Saiyid Sulaiman Nadvi presided. Resolutions were passed there condemning communal differences, urging Muhammadans to support the Congress and appealing for subscriptions.[17]

One highly disquieting feature in Indian politics at that time was the growing tension between the Hindus and the Muslims and consequent outbreak of communal riots at several places in India. The most terrible of these riots took place at Kohat in September 1924. Those events "proved unbearable" to Mahatma Gandhi and on the 18th September he imposed on himself a fast of twenty-one days, both as "penance and prayer" as he noted in the statement issued by him in this connection from Muhammad Ali's residence in Delhi on 18 September. A Unity Conference, presided over by Pandit Moti Lal Nehru and attended by three hundred delegates representing different schools of thought in the country including West Cott, the metropolitan of India, met at Delhi from 16 September. Authorised by the Conference, its president conveyed to Mahatma Gandhi its "united wishes" that he should immediately break his fast. But Mahatma Gandhi wrote in reply that he did not find it possible for him "to recall the fast". Sitting for several days the Unity Conference passed several resolutions for tolerance and communal goodwil. But these proved to be ineffective in steaming the tide of communal tensions. In fact, India became soon again the "playground of conflicting gusts of communal passions which resulted in numerous riots all over the country."[18]

Bihar did not escape the infection of communal frenzy, and in September-October 1924, Hindu-Muslim riots occurrde at several places in the province, the most serious one being at Bhagalpur. Rajendra Prasad and some other leaders ran there and did their best to ease the situation by staying there for a few days.[19]

An agreement, known as Calcutta Pact, was arrived at and published on the 6th November 1924, over the signatures of Mahatma Gandhi, Deshbandhu C.R. Das and Pandit Moti Lal Nehru. It ran as follows:

> "The Congress should resolve that different classes of work of the Congress may be done, as may be found necessary, by the different sections within the Congress and should resolve that the promotion of unity between the Hindus and Musalmans should be carried on by all sections within the Congress."[20]

The Bihar Provincial Congress Committee and the Khilafat Conference met at Purnea on the 5th and 6th December 1924. Srikrishna Sinha delivered his presidential address with touching eloquence dwelling on the major problems in the country and making, in conclusion, a special appeal for communal harmony and for onward march under the leadership of Mahatma Gandhi.[21]

During the revival of the Bihari Students' Conference in 1924, while addressing the preliminary meeting at Patna, Rajendra Prasad exhorted the audience to dedicate themselves to constructive work like Hindu-Muslim unity.[22]

Mahatma Gandhi's second Bihar tour began from 11 January 1927. At Gaya, Mahatma spoke on a request given by the Hindu Sabha during the suddhi work, "I have made no secret of the fact that I did not approve of all aspects of the 'Suddhi work'." After much prayerful study of the Hindu Shastras I have come to the conclusion that there is no room in them for conversions such as they have in Islam or Christianity. I am also certain on a prayerful reading of the Koran that there is no warrant for the tabligh that is being promoted tody. It is possible that I may be mistaken. Let God correct me in that case. I, for myself, would love to protect my religion with tapascharya the way of prayerful suffering, which is royal road to success in any noble object. The real memorial that the Hindus can raise to Swamiji, is to rid Hinduism of the curse of untouchability, let both Hindus and Musalmans cleanse their hearts with the purifying blood of Swamiji's sacrifice. I must be free to read the Gita or Koran of my own accord. Why should a Hindu compel me to read the one or a Musalman to read the other ? No one may stand between a man and his religion and God. He, who has no inkling of religion, whose heart is arid and unpurified, how dares he purify (by proselytising) others ? But that is my opinion. And as I am a votary of liberty, I have, in spite of my opinion, insisted that Shardanandji had as much right to propagate Vedic Dharmas as a Musalman to propagate that of the Koran. And if Shardanandji was assassinated for his Suddhi Work, it did not credit to Islam. Hinduism is proud of the sacrifice and had been enriched by it.

"Let no Musalman secretly approve of the fact or believe that it has done any good to Islam. Let not a single Hindu harbour any thought of retaliation. If the Hindu and the Musalman rid themselves of mutual distrust and fear, there is no power that can stop their freedom. We are the makers of our own slavery. I had sealed my lips up to now on this burning topic. It is Shardanandji's sacrifice that has compelled one to open them to a certain extent. But I can give no guidance in this atmosphere. I shall only send my prayers to God that He may rid of fear and hatred and distrust, and make us rely solely on the strength of love."[23]

On a special request Mahatma Gandhi spoke on Hindu-Muslim unity at Siwan in Hindi and observed, "God will one day make the Musalman and the Hindu do what they will not do today. If you are believers, I beseach you to retire into yourselves and pray to the Indweller to stay your hands from wrong and to make them do the right thing. Let us do our prayer every morning and evening. There is no other way."[24]

Party cleavage was no doubt a disintegrating factor in Indian National life in this period. The canker of communalism was also gnawing at it. Hindu-Muslim relations were far from cordial and communal riots broke out at several places, the most fierce being those in Calcutta during the month of April 1926. These had natural repercussions on the neighbouring province of Bihar, where also communal tension increased during April and May, resulting in some minor clashes here and there, e.g., at Sasaram and Shahabad, in Monghyr, in the Santhal Parganas, and on the borders of the districts of Muzaffarpur and Darbhanga. The general situation in the province, however, "became distinctly easier in the month of June and Bakr-Id festival passed off without grave disorder."[25] Conciliation Committees worked at several places to smoothen communal differences. Mazharul Haque, deeply mortified at the prevailing communal tension, took the lead in organising at Chhapra on 10 June 1926 a conference of prominent Congressmen of Bihar, some members of Khilafat Committee, and several others outside these two organisations.[26] After frank discussion for some days all present there expressed their determination to take adequate steps to check the evil effects of communal bitterness. According to the decision of the conference, Mazharul Haque, Maulvi Muhammad Shafi, Jagat Narayan Lal, Rajendra Prasad and some others began to tour in the province for this work. As a result of it, the atmosphere in Bihar remained comparatively free from the pernicious effects of communal riots,[27] but excitement continued.

Communal riots occurred at other places and the assassination of Swami Shardanand by a Muslim fanatic on 23 December 1926 shocked the country very much. It caused sensation in Bihar too and sympathisers observed hartal in his memory in most of its towns.[28] Mahatma Gandhi heard of this tragedy on his way to Gauhati, at Sorbhog, a wayside station, and observed, "He lived a hero. He had died a hero.... This tragedy has a national importance. It draws our pointed attention to an evil that is eating into the vitals of the nation. Both Hindus and Musalmans have the choice before them. We are both on our trial."[29]

When the Congress met at Gauhati on 26 December 1926, Mahatma Gandhi moved a resolution to "place on record its sense of the irreparable loss to the nation as sustained by the tragic death of the great Swamiji." Muhammad Ali seconded it. This Congress also passed the following resolution about Hindu-Muslim unity:

> "This Congress calls upon the Working Committee to take immediate action in consultation with Hindu and Musalman leaders to devise measures for the removal of the present deplorable differences between Hindus and Muslims."[30]

The murder of Swami Shardanand had caused a sensation in the province. The Hindus in most of the large towns observed Hartal, which were more or less complete, in his memory. The local press had extolled his virtues as a reformer and there had been some excited oratory on the side of the Arya Samajists against the Mohammadan community. Most of the leading Mohammadans had openly condemned the work of assassination, but this did not prevent the feelings between communities from becoming more bitter. Mourning processions, however, passed off without any unpleasant incidents.[31]

At Sasaram, there was serious Hindu-Muslim rioting early last year. More trouble had been threatened over the Basant Panchami festival. At Chakradharpur, the Raja of Prorahat, acting in a conciliatory manner, stopped the music of his daughter's wedding procession when passing by the mosque. The bridegroom party resented this and some of the local Marwaris also objected. There was some excitement in consequence, but the matter passed off, without serious disturbances.[32]

The month of June 1927 in Bihar was peaceful. Final report regarding the Bakr-Id shows that it passed over peacefully in 18 districts, riots only being reported in Patna,

Champaran, Saran and Gaya, the two latter being of minor importance.[33]

Further reports show that there was no trouble in connection with the Muharram. In some districts, e.g., Monghyr and Shahabad, Hindus entirely abstained from joining in the procession but in other places, in spite of the activities of the Hindu Sabha, Hindus participated. It was somewhat curious that in Bihar town in the Patna district where there had been some communal tension, Hindus joined freely in the celebration. In Gaya also, where there was trouble last year, Hindus assisted the Mohammadans to make the celebration a success.[34]

From Muzaffarpur it was reported that feeling between Hindus and Mohammadans was growing worse. In one village the Hindus prevented the Mohammadans from burying a corpse on land which the Mohammadans claimed as burial ground. The corpse was eventually buried with the assistance of the police and action under section 107 IPC was taken.[35]

The chief event of this fortnight was the serious communal riot at Bettiah. Arya Samajists were reported to have been showing increased activity in various parts of Bihar. In Monghyr, communal trouble nearly occurred in a village near the Darbhanga border owing to a Brahmin widow taking refuge with a Mohammadan.[36]

Many leaders in the country were eager to create united front against Government's attitude of uncompromisingness about the proposal for constitutional advance. S. Srinivas Iyengar, President, of the Congress, issued on the eve of the dissolution of the Assembly in New Delhi in March 1927, a fervent appeal laying considerable emphasis on the need for both political and communal unity.[37] About 30 prominent Muslim leaders met in a conference at New Delhi on 20 March 1927 and discussed about joint electorate.

A special meeting of the Muslim representatives of Bihar and Orissa was held on 8 May 1927, in the Anjuman-e-Islamia Hall at Patna to consider the Delhi proposals for joint electorate. Ali Imam, Maulana Shafi Daudi and Syed Abdul Aziz supported these. But some other prominent Muslim leaders led the opposition to the joint electorate. After prolonged discussion the following resolutions were adopted:[38]

> "In view of the fact that some leaders of the sister community are taking advantage of the proposals made at the Delhi Muslim Conference and there is danger that Muslims would be deprived of their rights of separate representation without their rightful demands being accepted and in view of the fact that separate representation of minorities was necessary so long as communalism reigned supreme in the country, and also in view of the fact that in spite of all sorts of friendly gestures on the part of Musalmans, the sister community has developed marked tendency towards communalism which is evident from its hostile attitude towards all political and religious rights of Musalmans and has recently been given public expression on the platform of the All-India Hindu Mahasabha at Patna, this conference of the Musalmans of Bihar and Orissa is of the opinion that the proposal for replacing separate electorate by mixed electorate are premature; and, as such, harmful to the interest of Musalmans and therefore this conference deprecates any attempt to take away the right of separate representation from Musalmans and declares that, in the circumstances mentioned above, the Musalmans are not at all prepared to give up the right of separate representation for any price. This Conference is of the opinion that reforms should at once be introduced in the North-Western Frontier Province and Sindh should at once be separated from Bombay Presidency and constituted into a separate Province and hopes that Hindus as a proof of their change of heart will support these demands of Musalmans and thus pave the way for settlement of political differences."[39]

However, a Unity Conference was held in Calcutta in October 1927, and passed resolutions in favour of a satisfactory solution of Hindu-Muslim problem. The All-India Congress Committee, meeting in Calcutta in the same month, also passed a resolution appealing to the Hindu and Muslim leaders to do their utmost to promote an atmosphere of cordiality in the country.[40]

With the inauguration of the Civil Disobedience Movement under the leadership of Mahatma Gandhi, 1930 proved to be one of the most eventful year, "a wonder year" in the history of our country. On 13 June 1930, Pandit Moti Lal Nehru and Syed Mahmood were arrested as acting President and Secretary of the Congress Working Committee, which was declared unlawful. The news of these arrests produced a thrill in the province of Bihar and hartal was observed at all important centres. One striking feature of the hartal at Patna that time was the closing of many Mohammadan shops whose owners had not joined the previous hartals. It may be noted here that Maulana Abul Kalam Azad's recent visit to Patna had produced a good effect, from national point of view, on the Muslims at Patna. Many youths among them started an organisation under the presidentship of Professor Abdul Bari with the object of popularising the idea of independence in their community.[41]

It is significant to note that besides the noble efforts of Hasan Imam to further the cause of nationalism, several other nationalist Muslims were also then doing their best to reinforce Muslim support and sympathy for it. Two largely attended conferences of nationalists were held at Patna on 15 and 16 July 1930, in which distinguished Muslim leaders like Maulana Husain Ahmad, Ahmad Sayeed, Ataullah Shah Bokhari and Siddiqui delivered impressive speech exhorting the Muslim to join the Congress.[42]

While the Delhi Settlement was under consideration, the country was confronted with grave internal problem. Communal madness had again triumphed over man's sanity to threaten seriously the unity of national struggle. Hindu-Muslim riots had broken out at some places—Agra, Banaras, Kanpur, Mirzapur and several other places. Their repercussions were apprehended in Bihar. But nothing serious happened here due to the unstinted efforts of Rajendra Prasad for the cause of communal harmony since his return to Patna from the Karachi Congress on the 7th April 1931, and the cooperation that he received from some prominent Muslim leaders of the Province. Besides issuing an appeal for this, it was decided to hold a preliminary meeting of the leading Hindus and Musalmans at Syed Abdul Aziz's residence in the evening of 9 April. The idea was to organise joint action to prevent communal trouble and to hold meetings at Patna and other places for propagating the message of concord and amity.[43]

It may be noted here that the 24th Session of the Bihari Students' Conference was held at Arrah on 17 and 18 October 1931.[44] Twenty-three resolutions were passed including the boycott of the evil of communalism.[45]

Meanwhile, the country had been in a state of suspense due to Mahatma Gandhi's fateful resolve to "fast unto death" on the question of the British Premier's Communal Award, published on 17 August 1932, giving separate electorate to the so-called Depressed Classes as in the case of the Muslims.[46]

An attempt was made before the enforcement of the provisions of the new Act to solve communal problems, through informal talks between the Congress President, Rajendra Prasad, and M.A. Jinah, President of the Muslim League, which continued for more than a month at Delhi. The object was to bring about an agreed so-called Communal Award and thus to minimise communal discord to enable the country to present a united front.[47]

The year 1935 saw a steady deterioration in communal relation chiefly owing to repercussions among the Muslims of the event in other province and the corresponding increased activity of the Hindu religious organisation. The year began in Bihar with fair prospect, which was soon deemed in February by the failure at Delhi of Rajendra Prasad-Jinah talks to effect any agreed communal settlement. The firing on a frenzied Muslim mob at Karachi on 19 March agitated the Muslim mind all over India and induced a desire for martyrdom that was not calculated to make the already strained relations with the major community any easier. Although the Bakr-Id in March passed off without serious trouble, rioting was narrowly averted at Kharagpur, Teghra and Shaikhpur in Monghyr district, while the sacrilegious defilement, with slaughtered calf's head, of a Devi Asthan outside Phenhara in Champaran was to bear its fruit of death five months later.[48]

In Bihar, however, there were some minor clashes here and there, except at Phenhara where on 4 August 1935, the situation became somewhat serious and the police, under orders of the Sub-divisional Officer, opened fire as a consequence of which some persons were killed and some were wounded. Sasaram had already begun to engage considerable attention of the political workers.[49]

In April, 7th day of Moharram happened to coincide with Ram Navami, which was celebrated with even larger Mahavir Jhanda processions than usual; a class of procession which throughout its few years' vogue had tended intensely to annoy Muslims who regarded it as a provocative substitute in which both communities used to join in happier years. The result was that the police and the magistracy almost everywhere had an anxious time; while several clashes between the communities took place at Hazaribagh and Ranchi. Although many persons, including policemen were injured at both these places.[50]

In the beginning of June 1935, there was somewhat unexpected outburst of Muslim feeling in Bihar as elsewhere, against clause 304 of the Government of India Bill before the House of Commons, which provided for future amendments in the method of election to the legislature.[51]

In August, the embitterment of communal relation brought tragedy in this Province. On 4 August 1935, very large crowds of armed Hindus, who had not forgotten the defilement of their Devi Asthan some five months before, assembled at Phenhara in Champaran ostensibly for a Mahavir Jhanda procession and broke the terms of compromise regarding the road of procession arrived at with the Muslims only two days previously. They then defied the repeated order of the Sadar Subdivisional Officer to disperse, attempted to invade the Muslim Idgah and compelled the S.D.O. to order the armed police to open fire, in the course of which 30 rounds were fired resulting in the death of six men and injuries to seven others. There were attempts in certain quarters to make communal and political capital out of the tragedy, but the prompt issue of communiques by Government foiled such attempts.

Again on 27 October 1936, there was a serious Hindu-Muslim clash over the old question of processions and music before the mosque. This time the scene was at Jamalpur in Monghyr district where an apparently in-offensive Muslim stranger was killed in the fracas.[53]

Anugrah Narayan Singh, General Secretary, Bihar Provincial Congress Committee, accompanied by Professor Abdul Bari, arrived at Aurangabad on 28 April 1937 at 9 A.M. when they were received by the leading citizens of this town both Hindus and Muslims at 3 P.M. The Mohammadans met Abdul Bari in his camp and chalked out a line of compromise and agreed to form a Conciliation Board.[54]

What was at one time feared to have developed in a serious situation, had been averted and communal harmony restored in the heart of Patna town by the tactful handling of the situation by the City Magistrate, Kripa Narayan Singh. It appeared that on May 12 two Muslims were found spitting in a temple in the city and a complaint was lodged against them but they were later on let off. Enraged at this, Hindus of the locality approached the Assistant Superintendent of Police, but failed to reach a compromise. But the City Magistrate pursued the path of compromise. A compromise petition signed by both the parties was filed and a complaint under section 295 I.P.C. and proceeding under section 107 and 117 Cr.P.C. were dropped by the City Magistrate.[55]

During the fortnight ending 26 June 1937, a meeting was held at Biharsharif under the presidentship of Anugraha Narayan Sinha, who, in his speech, emphasised the need of a national government for the redress of the sufferings of the people and urged for communal cooperation and harmony. It also passed the resolution regarding Hindu-Muslim unity.[56]

A well attended meeting of the Mohammadans of Bettiah town and Mufassil as well, in which the Hindus also took part, was addressed by Syed Mahmood and Maulana Wahhab Saheb of Darbhanga under the presidentship of Hafiz Sani of that place. Both of them during the course of their speeches dwelt upon two important points—firstly, Hindu-Mohammadan cooperation and hand-in-hand working for the cause of their country; and, secondly, the need of the Mohammadans towards joining the Congress unconditionally. They pointed out due to certain mischievous propaganda the Mohammadans were labouring under a delusion that the Hindus would take advantage over them and would provoke religious feeling in the long run if they came in or were entrusted with power and responsibility. Syed Mahmood cleared this position saying that the Congress was the institution working for the general mass without any consideration of caste and creed. "The Congress is of the poor and for the poor—Mohammadans and Hindus alike. Freedom of India means freedom of the Hindu and Musalman both."[57]

In view of a resolution of the Bihar Provincial Congress Committee, reconstituted during the fortnight ending 26 May 1937, a Muslim Mass Contact Sub-Committee was formed for wider mass contact. Efforts began to be made by this Sub-Committee and Congress workers in Bihar for enrolment of greater number of Muslims as members of the Congress.[58] The visit of Khan Abdul Ghaffar Khan to Bihar put a new life into the Muslim mass contact movement. He addressed meetings at Bankipur Maidan, at the Islamia Hall and at Madrasa Mosque at Chowk, Patna City, on 15, 20 and 21 July 1937. Meetings were largely attended by both the Muslims and Hindus. He explained in his meetings the expediency of joint efforts of both the communities to fight the British imperialism.[59]

It was very unfortunate that communalism was then developing in India as a very highly disruptive force in national life. Indeed, promotion of communal harmony was one of the principal aims of the Indian National Congress, and Ministry in Bihar was doing its best for it. The government here was determined that "any attempt to foment communal trouble should be strongly put down." Addressing the Bihar Legislative Assembly on 27 September 1937, Maurice Garnier Hallett observed, "I feel that even the short experience which we have had of the working of the new constitution during the present session goes to show that all minorities have a full opportunity of putting forward their views."[62]

But for some reason or other, passion occasionally rose high and there were communal friction and fracas, though mostly of minor nature here and there. Bihar's communal concord of earlier days being marred under certain forces. The outlook of the Muslim League became anti-Congress and its influence was now increasing in Bihar. The working committee of Bihar Muslim League met on 1 August 1937, and after criticising the representation of the Muslims in the Bihar Cabinet decided to invite Mohammad Ali Jinah to pay a visit to Patna to further the cause of the League. At a meeting of the Muslim League held on 22 September 1937, a resolution was passed against the recitation of Bande Matram as a national song and to ask Government to stop its singing at public meetings or in schools and colleges.[63]

Towards the end of October 1937, Jinah visited Bihar and his efforts to merge all Muslim parties here in the Muslim League resulted in the United Muslim Party and Ahrar Party joining the League. The negotiations between Jinah and Bihar Independent Muslim Party, which was the largest single Muslim group in the Legislature, broke down.[64]

But the Muslim League continued to make progress securing the adherence of greater number of Muslims and numerous meetings were held and some new branches of the League were formed. Jinah again came to Bihar and on 1 January 1938 he addressed a largely attended meeting at Gaya. The Muslim League also held two big meetings at Patna on 16 and 17 March 1938 with Syed Abdul Aziz as president and it thus claimed to have enrolled seventy thousand members in the Province of Bihar.[65]

The Muslim League Conference at Shaikhpura (Monghyr) was followed by another at Gaya on 23 April 1938, at which the Ministry was attacked in strong terms. The mass literacy and Muslim Mass Contact campaigns were particularly resented and also the grant of Rs. 10,000 for the uplift of Momins was "interpreted as an attempt to split the Mohammadan community."[66]

At Barh in the district of Patna, some stray cases of disturbances by some riff-raff had been reported in the town. It was rumoured that some externed goondas from outside had arrived there secretly inciting a section of Muslim community in various ways. Scenting the possibility of an undesirable development in future, some prominent citizens of the town, both Hindus and Mohammadans, convened a meeting which was presided over by B.K. Lal, Advocate. As a result, a Conciliation Board was formed for Hindu-Muslim unity.[67]

Another Muslim League Conference was held at Bihar on 15 and 16 May 1938, at which Syed Abdul Aziz presided. A movement claiming separate electorate for the Muslims in the Local Bodies was also on the increase and there was disorder among the students in educational institutions on the Bande Matram question.[68]

At Chhapra, the differences between the Hindus and the Mohammadan students over the singing of the Bande Matram song in Saran Academy had been brought to a happy close. A compromise had been arrived at between both the sections of the students and it had been accepted by school authority.[69]

In the month of June 1938, the Provincial League Executive issued a questionnaire to branch offices asking them to compile detailed information about the employment of Mohammadans in the administration and any instances in which discrimination was shown against Mohammadans. They also decided to establish a network of Anjumans or Ward Committees throughout the Province. Boycott of local election was continuing, and at a Subdivisional Conference at Samastipur on 19 June a resolution was passed to boycott the next District Board elections till separate electorates were formed. At Daltonganj there was boycott of Municipal election at the time by the Muslim Leaguers.[70] A new Urdu paper, entitled the 'Muslim League' appeared on 1 July 1938.[71] Numerous meetings were held by the members of League on 26 August 1938 to celebrate Palestine Day. There was deterioration in the communal situation in the months of July and August and disturbances took place at various places.

A communal trouble had been settled at Mohalla Bengabad in Gaya district. The reason for the trouble was that the potters of the locality had a 'Samadhi of a Bhagat' which they had been worshiping for a very long time. Recently they constructed a pucca platform round about the samadhi which so much enraged some Muslims that they wanted to destroy the Samadhi and the platform on the ground that the site was a Muslim graveyard. A complaint was referred before the S.D.O. who deputed Rai Sahib Chunnilal Rastogi, Honorary Magistrate to settle the dispute. Rai Sahib was able to settle the matter most amicably with the result that the Samadhi was allowed to remain intact and the new platform was curtailed a little. The compromise petition had been filed before the S.D.O.[72]

But good came out of evil. Bitterness of the spreading communal outbreaks in Bihar "produced a change of outlook towards the end of August", particularly among the Muslim League leaders.[73] At Siwan two communities spontaneously formed a conciliation committee and the same thing happened at Barbigha in the Monghyr district.[74] Government also noticed improvement in the communal situation in September.

With the object of organising peace brigade, a meeting of local workers was held in the Janata Office, Patna on 3 September 1938. It was decided that in view of the persistent rumour about communal disturbances and incitement by some undesirable persons to the end, the formation of peace brigade was necessary. The function of the brigade would be to go round all the Mohallas and counteract any propaganda which might rise communal passion and also to dispel the doubt and misunderstanding agitating the minds of the people by explaining to them the real situation.[75]

At Monghyr Mehdi Ali, Deputy Magistrate in charge of Barbigha and Shaikhpura area in the district of Monghyr to keep watch over the communal situation, had just started to report something very reassuring and happy about the way the Muslims and Hindus of Barbigha managed among themselves the Hindu and Muslim processions with complete accord and amity. Hindus joined in large number the huge

Muslims' demonstration on the 'Palestine Day' while Muslims in like numbers took active part in the Ganesh Puja processions.

In furtherence of the cause of Hindu-Muslim unity and restoration of good relation between the two communities, a stage performance was organised at the Badshah Nawab Rizvi Training College, Gulzarbagh, Patna through the efforts of Miss Veneta Husain, Principal of the College, and conducted entirely by the students of the college which centred exclusively to the education of girls, most of whom were Pardah-Nashin.[77]

But still numerous League meetings continued. Fazlul Haque, Premier of Bengal, presided at the 51st Session of the All-India Muslim Educational Conference at Patna on 1 and 2 October 1938. He criticised the educational policy of the Ministry and the Wardha Scheme of Education. His "excursion in the communal politics in the opening address and in other speeches", aroused "resentment among the Hindu press and public."[78]

The communal trouble then took place at Sultanganj in Monghyr district where Muslims levelled the charge of the cause of the riot against the Secretary and the President of Sultanganj Congress Committee. An emergent meeting of the Working Committee, Bhagalpur District Congress Committee, was held on 30 October 1938 under the presidentship of Rameshwar Narayan Agrawal at the Congress Office, Bhagalpur. It was resolved that a committee of 5 members, viz., Rameshwar Narayan Agrawal, Harkeshwar Prasad, Satrughan Prasad Singh, Subkaran Churibala and Maulvi Saufi Sahib should be formed to investigate the case of Sultanganj Hindu-Muslim riot and the charges levelled against the Secretary and the President of Sultanganj Congress Committee.[79]

The twenty-sixth Session of the All-India Muslim League met at Patna on 26 December 1938 and continued for the next three days under the presidentship of M.A. Jinah. The Chairman of the Reception Committee, S.A. Aziz, stressed in his speech the separate identity of the Musalmans, expressed "fear of the Musalmans that the Congress in reality wanted to establish Hindu Raj"[80] and enumerated their grievances. In his presidential address Jinah also observed, "The Congress High Command was determined to force their own culture on others and to establish a Hindu Raj".[81] As is noted in contemporary Government report[82], "there were many bellicose speeches". In moving a resolution against the federation, which was ultimately adopted, Maulana Zafar Ali Khan described it as a "monstrous political fraud imposed upon Indians". The resolution on direct action by the Muslims, which occupied almost the entire time of the second day's sitting of the League. In the course of debate many accusations were made against the Congress Governments, the chief object of attack being the Vidya Mandir Scheme, the Muslim mass contact campaign, Bande Matram, the National Flag, and Hindi as lingua franca. Charges of victimisation and operation were made against the Government. In a statement which the Minister of Education, Bihar, made in the Legislature, he explained that the general line of policy regarding Bande Matram should be optional and be limited to the first two times, which were considered to be non-controversial and that flag should be hoisted where the members of the managing committee and the boys decided to do so.[83]

All-India Muslim Students' Conference met at Patna on the 29th December 1938. It was inaugurated by Jinah and presided over by the Raja of Mahmudabad. There were some Muslim League Conferences and numerous Muslim League meetings at different places in Bihar throughout the year 1939. As regards the duties of the students, the Raja observed, "We are accused of isolating ourselves from other communities in our country and using fear and hatred as our weapons. It is for you, educated youngmen, to disprove the charge by deeds."[84]

There was intensification of Muslim League activity in Bihar, particularly in the enrolling and training of volunteers. Since the visit of Nazimuddin, Bengal Minister of Rajmahal in the Santhal Parganas district, the activities of the Muslim League extended to the Damin-Koh and volunteers were holding parades at Rajmahal, Sahebganj and Borio.[85]

At the Conference of the Bihar Provincial Muslim League, held at Patna on 12 March 1939, a resolution was passed that the Muslim League would start Civil Disobedience against the Government if the latter introduced the Wardha Scheme in the Province and the Conference of the All-India Muslim League to sanction the launching of civil disobedience.[86]

Number of investigating committees toured the country on behalf of the League and collected data which they published as charge against the Congress Government, which were not however substantiated.[87] The Bihar Congress Ministry, as the Congress Government in the other provinces, issued suitable replies to these and held that they were just in all respect to the minority community. It should also be noted that in Bihar there were then two other Muslim organisations, separate from the Muslim League and in opposition to that body. These were the Jamait-ul-Ulema and the Momin Jamait. At a Momin Conference, held at Darbhanga on 25 June 1939, the Momin put forward a demand for half the Muslim seats be allotted to the Momin community. There was a meeting of the Jamait-ul-Ulema at Bettiah in July 1939, in which the activities of the League were strongly condemned.

On 16 August 1939, on the assertion of the right by Muslims of village Konand in the district of Patna (now in Nalanda) to kill cows openly in their village and on their attempt to kill her in open maidan, the Hindus protested and the Muslims became furious and a riot broke up in which six persons received bullet wounds and sword injuries.[88]

Pandit Baleshwar Jha, Pleader, Secretary, Subdivisional Hindu Mahasabha, Samastipur wrote: The year 1939, it was the ninth anniversary of the Shankar Dal which fell on August 20, 1939. After having obtained license for the procession, it started at about 2 P.M. from the local Thaneshwar Asthan. There was very large gathering of about 7-8 thousand of Hindus. The procession passed through the Juma Masjid road at about 2.30 P.M. and all along at about 6 P.M. When the procession passed through Gurdari Bazar lane on its return journey, there was heavy downpour, but the procession proceeded. During the rain some 8 or 10 villagers, who were sight-seers, left the procession at the eastern entrance of Gurdari Bazar. In order to reach home earlier they went through Juma Masjid road. When these poor people reached near the Masjid, some 15 Musalmans wanted to start a riot. One Nabi Mian, it is alleged, ordered them to beat the Hindu passersby saying that that was not the road Hindu. Unfortunately one Lakhan Raut was hit with brickbat which resulted in injury. Thus the Hindu-Muslim riot began.[89]

A trouble over alleged injuries on a dedicated bull in village Jian Sadar P.S. in the district of Muzaffarpur, which threatened to assume an ugly communal outlook between Hindus and Muslims was very tactfully averted by the prompt action of S.I., Jabbar of Sadar P.S., who rushed to the scene immediately on receiving information.[90]

At the instance of K.N. Singh, S.D.O., Giridh, the influential representative of both the communities met on 10 October 1939 in the court verandah and discussed ways for maintaining peace during the ensuing Puja celebrations. The S.D.O. requested both the communities to eschew all ill-will and malice and to entertain a spirit of tolerance. He advised Muslims to allow Hindus to do whatever they liked and threw the burden on the Hindus to see that they did not injure the feelings of the Muslims in any way. This spirit, he said, was the best method of avoiding a clash and effacing malice. The Muslims agreed to this, whereupon the Hindu representatives declared in the meeting that when the Muslims have left the responsibility on them, it would be their solemn duty to discharge it and to try their level best to see that Muslims' feelings are not wounded.[91]

Much relief was noticed and towards the close of the meeting two Conciliation Boards for Giridih and Pachamba, comprising of select representatives, were formed. Nageshwar Prasad Sinha and Girbardhari Prasad were authorised to act as Secretaries of the respective Boards. These Boards would make all possible efforts to keep the situation under control.[92]

To prevent the communal riots in the Hazaribagh district, a Conciliatory Committee representative of all communities and parties was formed. A public meeting held on 5 October 1939, over which the Deputy Commissioner of Hazaribagh presided. Khan Sahib Syed Gholam Jilani, S.D.O., Sadar and Mr. Chhatradhari Prasad were elected Joint Honorary Secretaries.[93]

At Gaya, with the approach of Dashahara, the police and the executive officer were having a busy time and taking all possible precautions to ensure its due celebration without any disturbances. B.N. Singh, District Magistrate, convened a meeting of the leading Hindus and Muslims in the chamber with a view to invite suggestions regarding processions. Muslims suggested that the procession should pass the Juma Masjid after 10 P.M. this time as, owing to Ramazan, there would be prayers and Taravih till that time. The District Magistrate, after hearing both the parties, referred the matter to the already existing Conciliation Board, which was formed there during the last communal riot, making the members responsible for peace and safety of the town and asking for a report from them. The Conciliation Board met and agreed to let the processions pass the Juma Masjid after the prayers and Taravih were over. They had also taken upon themselves the task of trying to maintain peace in the town and reply to this effect had been sent to the District Magistrate.[94]

A communal riot broke out on 22 October 1939 at Balia in Begusarai Subdivision near the mosque at about the time of immersion of the Durga idol. The Subdivisional Officer and the Police Inspector with an armed force were at the spot but the situation was under control.[95]

From an information received in Patna from Daltonganj, it appears that there was some trouble in Haider Bazar while the Dashahara procession was passing through a mosque, and a communal riot was narrowly averted and military police reached Haider Nagar.[96]

A meeting of the Hindu-Muslim Reconciliation Board was held at the Dak Bungalow Balia in Begusarai Subdivision under the presidentship of A.N.M. Omar, S.D.O., Begusarai on 26 October 1939. Members of both communities were present. A Sub-Committee, consisting of Messrs. Brahmdeo Narayan Sinha, M.L.A., Choudhary Enamul Haque alias

Matlub Babu, Abdul Khalid and Raghunandan Lal, was formed to investigate the minimum demands of the members of the two communities and to make recommendations on the subject as early as possible within a week. Another Sub-Committee was formed to investigate into the rumours and reports intended to flare up communal disturbance and to take prompt steps to remove the misunderstanding. Members of the Sub-Committee were Bhakari Lal, Rameshwar Lal Rastogi, Mohammad Ashique and Hakim Naziruddin.[97]

At Barh, on 23 October 1939, the image of Durga passed in a procession through the main streets. On one of the flanks of the Thana Compound besides the Garden Street is situated a mosque, and the procession passed through that road as usual. The local police were in attendance. Yet some undesirable elements on either sides sought to create disturbances but the local police formed themselves into a cordon between the undesirable group of each side and succeeded in preventing any untoward incident.[98]

The Mohammadans of Nawada under the guidance of Mr. A.H. Khan, S.D.O., from whom this idea originated, gave a remarkable demonstration of goodwill towards Hindu brethren and encouraging scenes of communal amity. When, on the occasion of Id, they were at home, about 400 Hindu guests from all parts of the district were invited. The school compound was gaily decorated and excellent arrangements were made in orthodox and non-orthodox styles.[99]

Addressing a crowded meeting of the people of Dehri Thana, Rang Bahadur Prasad stressed the need for communal amity and fervently appealed to Hindus and Muslims to shed their differences in the cause of motherland and rally round the banner of freedom.[100]

Jaglal Choudhary was continuing his propaganda tour in the Purnea district. He was exhorting the people to create mutual goodwill and communal harmony. He toured Kishanganj, Bishunpur Hal (P.S. Bahadurganj), Hathimara (P.S. Kishanganj), Islampur Chapra.[101]

The Bihar Government issued a press note. At about 9 A.M. on 19 November 1939 the Hindus of Kishanganj in the district of Purnea took out a Gopastmi procession after taking proper license. But the trouble began.

A communal riot occurred in village Banauli, about 2 miles from Bihar Town in Patna district. On 19 November 1939, Hindus are said to be assaulted.[102]

While presiding the Purnea District Political Conference on 16 and 17 December 1939, S.K, Sinha, Bihar complemented the Purnea Hindus and Musalmans on their cordial relations and cited it an object of lesson to other restless communalists who were proving a stumbling block in the path of progress.[103]

At a public meeting held in the public library at Nawada, a Peace Committee was formed to adopt measures to promote communal harmony throughout the Subdivision. It was resolved to award medals as follows:

(i) Two gold medals to two gentlemen of the Subdivision who will make best efforts in promoting communal harmony throughout the Subdivision.

(ii) Two silver medals to two gentlemen in each thana who will make best efforts to keep peace in coming Bakr-Id festival in the Subdivision.

The medals will be awarded by the Peace Committee on behalf of the public of Nawada Subdivision.

A committee was formed of which the office-bearers were elected as follows:

President	A.H. Khan, S.D.O.
Secretary	S.N. Haider
Treasurer	S.C. Jain

About 200 rupees were promised as a donation by others, who were present.[104]

To conclude, it can be said that one highly disquieting feature in Indian politics during the period of study was the growing tension between the Hindus and Muslims and consequent outbreak of communal riots in different parts of India. Bihar did not escape the infection of communal frenzy and

Hindu-Muslim riots occurred at several places during this period. Rajendra Prasad and some other leaders of both the communities laboured hard to lessen the communal differences. They toured the affected areas, organised conciliation committees and unity conferences and addressed meetings appealing to the people to sink their petty differences in the interest of the nation. As a result, the atmosphere in Bihar remained comparatively free from the pernicious effects of communal riots, though the tension continued to prevail at some places.

References

1. Datta, K.K., *History of the Freedom Movement in Bihar*, Vol. I, p. 368.
2. *1921 Movement*, Forwarded by V.V. Giri, p. 17.
   Singh, Anugraha Narayan, *Mere Sansmaran*, p. 28.
3. *Young India (1919-27)*, Edited by Gandhiji, p. 152.
4. *Political Special File No. 44/1921*, Bihar State Archives, Patna.
5. *Political Special File No. 244/1921*, Bihar State Archives, Patna.
6. Ibid.
7. Ibid.
8. Ibid.
9. Ibid.
10. Ibid.
11. Ibid., *Extract from D.I.G. Weekly Report* for June 12, 1921.
12. *The Non-Cooperation and Khilafat Movement in Bihar and Orissa*, p. 60.
13. Ibid., pp. 59-60.
14. Singh, Anugraha Narayan, *Mere Sansmaran*, p. 39.
15. Datta, K.K., *History of the Freedom Movement in Bihar*, Vol. I, p. 409.
16. Prasad, Rajendra, *An Autobiography*, pp. 163-64.
17. *The Non-Cooperation and Khilafat Movement in Bihar and Orissa*, pp. 131-35.
18. Prasad, Rajendra, *Atmakatha*, p. 236.
19. *Young India* in 1925-26, Introduction by Rajendra Prasad, XXVIII.
20. Datta, K.K., *History of the Freedom Movement in Bihar*, Vol. I, p. 460.
21. *The Non-Cooperation and Khilafat Movement in Bihar and Orissa*, pp. 144-45.
22. *The Searchlight*, April 11, 1924.

23. *Young India, 1927-28*, pp. 58-59.
24. Ibid., pp. 65-67.
25. *Bihar and Orissa in 1926-27*, p. 7.
26. *The Indian Quarterly Report*, 1926, Vol. I, p. 16.
27. Ibid.
28. *Bihar and Orissa in 1926-27* p. 7.
29. Tendulkar, *Mahatma*, Vol. II, p. 314.
30. Datta, K.K., *History of the Freedom Movement in Bihar*, Vol. I, p. 498.
31. *Fortnightly Report of the Government of India, Home Deptt.*, for the first half of January 1927.
32. Ibid., for the second half of January 1927.
33. Ibid., for the second half of June 1927.
34. Ibid., for the second half of July 1927.
35. Ibid.
36. Ibid., for the first half of August 1927.
37. *Indian Quarterly Register*, 1927, Vol. I, pp. 33-34.
38. Ibid., pp. 39-40.
39. Datta, K.K , *History of the Freedom Movement in Bihar*, Vol. I, p. 500.
40. Ibid.
41. *Report of the Provincial Congress Committee*, for the week ending July 4, 1930.
42. *The Searchlight*, July 17, 1930.
43. Ibid., April 10, 1931.
44. Datta, K.K., *History of the Freedom Movement in Bihar*, Vol. II, p. 163.
45. *Weekly Report of the Superintendent of Police*, *Shahabad*, October 23, 1931
46. Datta, K.K., *History of the Freedom Movement in Bihar*, Vol. II, p. 190.
47. *The Searchlight*, Sept. 21, 1932.
48. *The Indian Nation*, March 8, 1935; *Extract from Bihar and Orissa Government Administration Report*.
49. Datta, K.K., *History of the Freedom Movement in Bihar*, Vol. II, p. 291.
50. *The Indian Nation*, April 18, 1935; *Extract from Bihar and Orissa Government Administration Report*.
51. Ibid.
52. *Extract from Bihar and Orissa Government Report*.
53. Ibid.
54. *The Indian Nation*, April 29, 1937.
55. Ibid., June 9, 1937.
56. *Letter from District Magistrate of Patna to Commissioner*, Patna Division, dated June 26, 1937.
57. *The Indian Nation*, June 27, 1937.

58. *Report of the District Magistrate to the Commissioner*, Patna Division, for the period ending May 26, 1937.
59. Ibid., for the period ending July 25, 1937.
60. *Report of the Dist. Magistrate, Shahabad to Commissioner*, Patna Division, August 11, 1937.
61. *Letters from the Chief Secretary, Bihar to the Commissioner*, Patna Division, August 20, 1937.
62. *The Indian Nation*, September 2[illegible], 1937.
63. *Report from the Magistrate of Patna to the Commissioner*, Patna Division, October 12, 1937.
64. Ibid., for the second half of October 1937.
65. *Report on Political Events* during the second half of March 1938.
66. Ibid., for the second half of April 1938.
67. *The Indian Nation*, May 3, 1938.
68. *Report on Political Events* during the second half of April 1938.
69. *The Indian Nation*, May 14, 1938.
70. *Report on Political Events* during the second half of June 1938.
71. Ibid., during the first half of July 1938.
72. *The Indian Nation*, July 17, 1938.
73. *Report on Political Events* during the first half of September 1938.
74. Ibid.
75. *The Indian Nation*, September 4, 1938.
76. Ibid., September 7, 1938.
77. Ibid., September 23, 1938.
78. *Report on Political Events* during the first half of Oct. 1938.
79. *The Indian Nation*, November 3, 1938.
80. *The Indian Annual Register*, 1938, Vol. II, p. 343.
81. Ibid., pp. 344-45.
82. *Report on Political Events in Bihar* during the second half of December 1938.
83. Ibid.
84. Datta, K.K., *History of the Freedom Movement in Bihar*, Vol. II, p. 335.
85. Ibid., p. 336.
86. *The Indian National Register*, 1939, Vol. I, p. 371.
87. Prasad, Rajendra, *India Divided*, pp. 146-65.
88. *The Indian Nation*, August 18, 1939.
89. Ibid., August 31, 1939.
90. Ibid., September 14, 1939.
91. Ibid., October 10, 1939.
92. Ibid.
93. Ibid., October 11, 1939.
94. Ibid., October 20, 1939.
95. Ibid., October 23, 1939.

96. Ibid., October 25, 1939.
97. Ibid., October 31, 1939.
98. Ibid., November 1, 1939.
99. Ibid., November 18, 1939.
100. Ibid.
101. Ibid., November 30, 1939.
102. Ibid., December 4, 1939.
103. Ibid., December 22, 1939.
104. Ibid., December 30, 1939.

6

Removal of Untouchability

The year 1921 is regarded as having witnessed the first non-cooperation or civil disobedience movement started by Mahatma Gandhi for winning of freedom of the country. The occasion was to concentrate on constructive programmes, such as, removal of untouchability.[1]

Meeting at Delhi on 4 and 5 November 1921, the All-India Congress Committee authorised "every province, on its own responsibility, to undertake Civil Disobedience including non-payment of taxes." The conditions were many but one of them was that in the event of individual civil disobedience the individual "must be a believer in Hindu-Muslim unity and in unity among all the communities professing different religions in India as an article of faith."

Soon after returning from Ahmedabad, the prominent Bihar delegates began to consider how best they could carry out the latest instruction of the Congress. A fairly representative meeting of the Provincial Congress Committee was held at Patna on 5 January 1922 to discuss future plan of action in the light of the Ahmedabad resolution. The following instructions were issued to the District Congress Committees:

"1. The union among Hindus, Muslims and other communities should be strengthened so that men of all castes and creeds be of one heart.
2. Among the Hindus, those castes which are regarded as 'untouchables' should not be looked down upon nor physical contact with them be considered objectionable."[2]

The Working Committee of the All-India Congress met at Bardoli on 11 and 12 February 1922, passed a resolution suspending mass civil disobedience movement and directed the Congress organisation to "concentrate on constructive activity like improving the condition of the depressed classes."

To push forward the constructive activities according to the ideas of Mahatma Gandhi an organisation, called the Gandhi Seva Sangh, was started in 1923. Rajagopalachari, Sardar Vallabhbhai Patel, Gangadhar Rao Deshpande, Seth Jamnalal Bajaj, Rajendra Prasad and others became members of its executive. Its branches were started in Bihar. But no centre was established for its work. Later on attempts were made in this direction at village Mairva in Saran district, but it did not prove fruitful.[3]

Before the close of the year 1923 the different political bodies in Bihar discussed some significant matters. The Bihar Provincial Conference met at Motihari on 31 October and 1 November 1923 under the presidentship of Dharnidhar of Darbhanga. Gorakh Prasad was chairman of the Reception Committee. It was attended by a large audience and Deva Das Gandhi was also present on this occasion. Resolutions were passed re-affirming faith in Mahatma Gandhi's ideals. In his speech, the President emphasised on constructive work.[4]

With the efforts of Ram Prasad, an organisation called Patna Seva Sangh had been started in Patna. The Sangh would work for:

1. The establishment of relationship of love, mutual goodwil and amity amongst the different sections of

the people and would always endeavour to remove causes of friction between different castes and classes of the Indian community.

2. The removal, as far as possible, of the distress of the poor, the famished, the widow and the otherwise destitute.
3. The betterment of the condition of the depressed classes and other progress towards higher and greater life.[5]

An agreement, known as "Calcutta Pact" arrived on 6 November 1924, over the signature of Mahatma Gandhi, Deshbandhu C.R. Das and Pandit Motilal Nehru. It ran as follows:

"The Congress should resolve that different classes of work of the Congress may be done by the different sections within the Congress and should resolve that the promotion of unity between the Hindus and the Musalmans and the removal of untouchability by the Hindus from amongst them, should be carried on by all sections within the Congress."[6]

While addressing the preliminary meeting of the Bihari Students' Conference at Patna in April 1924, Rajendra Prasad exhorted the audience to dedicate themselves to constructive work like removal of untouchability and education of the untouchables in night schools, etc.[7]

Mahatma Gandhi's second Bihar tour, which was remarkable from the point of view of removal of untouchability, began from 11 January 1927. At Gaya, the municipality presented an address to Mahatma Gandhi, which was sceptical about untouchability programme. There the Hindu Sabha gave an address to him, which besides expressing heartiest sympathy with untouchability, requested him to bless their Suddhi work. His reply to them was:[8]

"I have made no secret of the fact that I did not approve of all aspects of the 'Suddhi work'. After much prayerful study of the Hindu Shastras I have come to the conclusion that there is no room in them for conversions, such as they have in Islam and Christianity. I am also certain on a prayerful reading of the Quran that there is no warrant for the tabligh that is being promoted today. It is possible that I may be mistaken. Let God correct me in that case. I for myself would love to protect my religion with tapascharya, the way of prayerful suffering, which is the royal road to success in any noble object. The real memorial that the Hindus can raise to Swamiji is to rid Hinduism of the curse of untouchability. Let both Hindus and Musalmans cleanse their heart with the purifying blood of Swamiji's sacrifice. I must be free to read the Gita or the Quran of my own accord. Why should a Hindu compel me to read the one or a Musalman to read the other? Why should I need a Christian to compel me to read the Bible? No one may stand between a man and his religion or God. He who has no inkling of religion, whose heart is arid and unpurified, how dare he purify (by proselytising) others? But that is my opinion. And as I am a votary of liberty, I have, in spite of my opinion, insisted that Shardhanandjee had as much right to propagate Vedic Dharma and a Musalman propagates Quran. And if Shardhanandji was assassinated for his Suddhi work, it did not credit to Islam. Hinduism is proud of the sacrifice and had been enriched by it.

"Let no Musalman secretly approve of the fact or believe that it has done any good to Islam. Let not a single Hindu harbour any thought of retaliation. If the Hindu and the Musalman rid themselves of mutual distrust and fear, there is no power that can stop their freedom. We are the makers of our own slavery. I had sealed my lips up to now on this burning topic. It is Shardhanandji's sacrifice that has compelled me to open them to a certain extent. But I can give no guidance in this atmosphere. I shall only send my prayers to God that He may rid us of fear and hatred and distrust, and make us rely solely on the strength of love."[9]

The Congress at its Calcutta session of 29 December 1928, passed a resolution outlining future programme of constructive work for Congressmen, in the Legislatures and outside. Such works were—eradication of social abuses and encouragement of women to take their due share in national upbuilding, removal of untouchability and various disabilities of the so-called untouchables.

In Bihar, there was some relaxation in the rigour of untouchability. Children of the so-called untouchables were admitted into schools. Generally they were getting access to wells, a number of men were ceasing to have any objection to water and even food being touched by them. The following incidents may be noted in this connection:

(a) A Dusadh arranged Satyanarayan Katha at Patna and some respectable gentlemen of other castes took sweets on this occasion.[10]

(b) At Motihari, a Chamar joined Katchi Dinner with men of Brahman, Bhumihar Brahman, Rajputs, Kayastha and some other castes.[11]

(c) At the Arya Samaj Anniversary at Dinapur, where Rajendra Prasad presided and Raja Saheb of Kalakankar as well as the Kumar Saheb of Amethi were present, Brahman and Sudras of both the sexes took water from a Dom (sweeper).[12] Some people of Champaran and Muzaffarpur also organised inter-caste dinner.[13]

With the inauguration of the Civil Disobedience movement under the leadership of Mahatma Gandhi, 1930 proved to be one of the most eventful years, "a wonder year" in the history of our country. Bihar Provincial Congress Committee issued[14] on 20 January 1930, many programmes for the celebration of the Independence Day on 26 January next. One of them was to work for the upliftment of untouchables, e.g., taking them into the temples, allowing them to free use of wells, etc.

On April 9, 1930, Mahatma Gandhi circulated the following directions:

"Let every village fetch or manufacture contraband salt. Sister should picket liquor shops. Hindu should eschew untouchability."[15] These directions proved fruitful.

As many as 250 sweepers of the Manbhum Municipality had now given up their drinking habit and had been brought under social organisation of their own by the sole efforts of Girish Chandra Mazumdar. Five months ago, they were to be seen in the evenings to roll down on the streets in a miserable state of drunkenness, but since reclamation work had been taken in hand, they occupy themselves in their off-house with Harisankritan, Ramayan and Mahabharat reading and attending night school. Three schools had been opened for their boys and girls to learn alphabet. A short cooperative movement had been started for them to relieve them from the ethics of unscrupulous mahajans and they deposited money out of their own pay every month at a rate varying from Re. 1 to Rs. 3 and took loans from this fund in case of extreme necessity. Jimut Bahan Sen was trying to introduce Charkha work among the sweepers.[16]

The Working Committee of the Bihar Provincial Congress Committee had appointed Bindeshwari Prasad Verma, the President of the Congress Committee, Muzaffarpur to carry on the work of the removal of untouchability in the province and carry on propaganda to get temples, wells, dharamshala, etc., thrown open to untouchables.[17]

It may be noted here that the 24th Session of the Bihari Students' Conference was held at Arrah on 17 and 18 October 1931. Twenty-three resolutions were passed, such as, providing opportunity to the student to come in contact with the villagers for educating them in matters like untouchability and boycott the evil of communalism.[18]

At the request of Bindeshwari Prasad Verma, Member Incharge, Untouchability Department of the Bihar Provincial Congress Committee, the Mahanth of Chaturbhuj Asthan, a famous temple of the province, had allowed all the untouchables and the members of the depressed classes entered the temple without any distinction.[19]

The Paru Thana Congress Committee concluded its session at Fatehabad under the presidentship of Narayan Prasad. Speeches were delivered laying stress on the removal of untouchability.[20]

One remarkable effect of Mahatma Gandhi's fast was to set in motion effectual forces throughout the country for removal of untouchability. Rajendra Prasad had stated: "The Hindu society is on its trial, and if it has any life in it, it must now respond with great and magnificent act." In a speech delivered by Gurudeo Rabindranath at Poona on 27 September 1932, the sixty-fourth b rthday of Mahatma Gandhi, he thus appealed to the heart of the nation for this work in his own unique way. "Today in our determined effort, let us all join Mahatmaji", the poet observed, "in his noble task of removing the burden of the ages, the burden of disrespect upon the bent back of those who have been stimatized for the accident of their birth, and the sinful denial to large body of our countrymen, of sympathy which is the birth right of all human beings. We are not only casting off the chain of India's moral enslavement but indicating the path for all humanity. We are challenging the victimization, however and in whatever form it exists, to stand the test of relentless questioning of conscience with Mahatmaji has brought to bear upon our day."[21]

Chait Shankranti, a well-known Hindu festival, was celebrated at Tilothu by the students of local high school. Pandit Nityanand Pathak, Sahityacharya, delivered an able speech during the course of which he urged the students to treat along the footprints of Ram Chandra in all matters including the removal of untouchability for which the great teacher had set an example by accepting plums from the hands of Sabari, a woman of low caste.[22]

At Chhapra it was proposed to prepare a number of huts for Harijans who were shelterless. Syed Mahmood had arranged to get nearly 50 huts prepared, each for a family in Chhapra town,and 21 huts were under construction in the Nayi Bazar for them. These were being constructed on the scheme of Dr. Soor which included bathrooms and a fine park near the huts to be used exclusively by them. Swami Yoganandji with his band of workers was getting the huts constructed. After the construction of these, huts would be prepared in other parts of the town.[23]

The Harijan Movement was active in Giridih. A Harijan Board had been constituted and it had been affiliated to the Provincial Harijan Board. Very recently a Harijan School had been established and it was progressing.[24]

Progressive social revolution in our country was taking place for adjustment to changing circumstances. Untouchability Abolition Week was observed from 27 September to 3 October, and on 30 September the All-India Anti-Untouchability League was inaugurated. It had its headquarters at Delhi with Amrit Lal V. Thakkar as its Secretary. Its branches were soon started at different provincial centres.[25]

Bihar's response in this respect was splendid. Here, work of upliftment of the depressed class, or the Harijans as Mahatma Gandhi called them, had already begun. On 17 July 1932, a meeting was held in the Model School at Gaya for this purpose. A Mehtar (sweeper) of Gaya addressed this meeting and distributed Elaichi and Supari (betelnut) to the audience, most of these took these.[26] In fact, several meetings were held at Gaya, Nawada and Aurangabad which were attended both by the caste Hindus and depressed classes and attempts were made by the former to embrace the latter.[27]

In the Patna district, such meetings were held at Patna City, Barh, Mokameh, Bakhtiyarpur, Bihar, Dinapur, Bihta, Maner, Khagaul and Bikram.[28] In the Shahabad district, similar meetings were held about the middle of September 1932 at Arrah, Buxar, Bhabhua and Durgauti.[29] Efforts were made for opening the temples to depressed classes successfully at some places, viz., Berhampur temple in Shahabad and at Jamhor in Aurangabad, though there was opposition also here and there from the more orthodox people. At Arrah another meeting was organised on 25 September 1932 in front of the temple of one Rameshwar Prasad, a retired Peshkar of the Collectorate. After Puja (worship) of Satyanarayanji, 'prashad' was distributed and some mild resolutions were passed.[31]

Another meeting was held there at 5.30 P.M. on 26 September 1932. The audience offered a prayer for the life of Mahatma Gandhi and dispersed amidst cries of 'Shanti', 'Mahatma Gandhi ki Jai', 'Swatantra Bharat ki Jai'. There was a third meeting at Arrah on 27 September 1932 under the presidentship of Chandra Shekhar Prasad Singh of Chougain, who announced there the acceptance of the Poona Agreement and the breaking of Mahatma Gandhi's fast and impressed upon the audience the need of loving their brethren of the depressed classes. During the month of October 1932, there were meetings at many places in the different districts for the removal of untouchability,[32] opinion in favour of which was generally growing strong in spite of opposition from some people of orthodox views here and there.

A provincial organisation for anti-untouchability work soon came into existence in Bihar. An Anti-Untouchability Conference was held on 6 November 1932, in the Anjuman-e-Islamia Hall, Patna, with Radhika Raman Prasad Sinha of Surajpura as its president. Pandit Brij Bihari Chaube, an eminent Ayurvedic Physician of Bihar, and Chairman of the Reception Committee for this function, delivered an appealing speech stressing the need of eradicating the evil of untouchability which was eating into the vitals of the Hindu society. The president exhorted the Caste Hindus to treat the so-called untouchables properly and to afford them all facilities for their social and educational uplift. Amrit Lal V. Thakkar and Rajendra Prasad were also present at that meeting.[33] The following five resolutions were passed there:

"1. That the Hindus do away with the curse of untouchability and manifold evils which have crept into Hindu society and are eating into vitals, splitting up into various sections, making it weak, disunited and disintegrated, and as a result of which so many of God's creatures have been denied opportunities for physical, mental, social and spiritual development and Hindu society has been disgressed in the eye of the world.

That Caste Hindus should themselves through opening the wells, temples and tanks without any restriction to the untouchables and get others over whom they have influence to do the same.

3. That Depressed Classes should help the movement by introducing necessary reforms among themselves in the matter of their own living, eating, and drinking, etc.
4. That the Local Government and the Municipal and District Board authorities should be requested to help by stipends, contributions and other facilities for untouchables' promotion of their social welfare.
5. That a Provincial Board of the Anti-Untouchability League be formed and affiliated to the All-India League."

Pandit Brij Bihari Chaube, Radhika Raman Prasad Sinha, Roy Brij Raj Krishna and Vijoy Singh became Vice-Presidents of this Board. Bindeshwari Prasad Verma and Ram Chandra Pandit became its secretary and treasurer respectively.[34]

The Government of Bihar & Orissa did not "approve of government servants joining anti-untouchability league."[35] But it had behind it popular enthusiasm which was the most favourable factor for the success of any scheme of social reform. The record of its work from 6 November 1932 to 30 September 1933, as reported by its Secretary, was as follows:[36]

The Bihar Provincial Board was formed on 6 November 1932. Since then the following 14 district committees had been organised: Patna, Gaya, Arrah, Bhagalpur, Monghyr, Muzaffarpur, Champaran, Darbhanga, Santhal Parganas, Saran, Purnea, Ranchi, Hazaribagh and Purulia. The question of opening the 15th committee for Palamau was under consideration.

Besides the Provincial Anti-Untouchability Conference held at Patna at which our General Secretary, A.V. Thakkar, was himself present there were six District Conferences at Chhapra, Arrah, Bhagalpur, Monghyr, Jehanabad and Bettiah all of which excepting the last were attended by the Provincial Secretary.

Pandit Indra Raman Shastri, a known scholar, one of the signatories to the famous Poona 'Vyavastha' very kindly visited Jehanabad, Gaya, Arrah, Patna and Deoghar and delivered impressive lectures. Special propaganda against untouchability was carried on by Muzaffarpur District Committee in Sonepur Fair, Ramnavami Mela at Sitamarhi and Susta Mela, and by the Arrah Committee at Berahimpur Mela by organising lectures and distributing handbills and leaflets.

All the three Harijan Days were observed throughout the Province. On these days the functions were celebrated in almost all the towns and hundreds of villages, and the Caste Hindus and Harijans fraternised everywhere very liberally in various ways during the three weeks' fast of Mahatma Gandhi, the 21 days were observed in all important places in various ways by holding meetings, offering prayers, taking out processions and kirtan parties, organising joint sports, awarding prizes, cleaning Harjan colonies, collecting funds, feasting Harijans, etc.

The presidential speeches of Radhika Raman Prasad Sinha and Bhagwan Das at Patna and Chhapra conferences respectively had been reprinted. A Hindi version of the Constitution of Servants of the Untouchables Society's 'Blue Book' had been published. Ten thousand copies of 'Shastriyon ki Uvavastha' were printed for general distribution. A special appeal to the trustees of temples had also been issued. Magic lantern lectures were also given at several places in the district of Muzaffarpur.

In the district of Ranchi, Hazaribagh and Manbhum, there is very little objection to the Harijans entering temples. In other places 236 temples were opened to Harijans. There were 257 joint religious kirtans, kathas, bhajans and prayers. One new temple had been opened under the name of 'Patit Pavan Bhagwan' in Colong, district Bhagalpur, and another was under construction in Mohalla Mendichak, Bhagalpur.

The following District Committees were granting monthly stipends as per detail below:

Monghyr	15.12.0
Arrah	6
Bhagalpur	7
Darbhanga	25
Hazaribagh	1
Gaya	1

The Patna District Committee maintains one and the Darbhanga Committee maintains two students who were preparing for admission to the H.E. School.

The Provincial Office was granting 4 scholarships amounting to Rs. 17 per month.

The Raghumal Trust scholarship of Rs. 45 per month had been distributed among the districts as follows:

Bhagalpur	Rs. 3
Muzaffarpur	Rs. 3
Patna	Rs. 4
Hazaribagh	Rs. 6
Deoghar	Rs. 3
Ranchi	Rs. 4
Purnea	Rs. 3
Saran	Rs. 3
Darbhanga	Rs. 4
Gaya	Rs. 3
Champaran	Rs. 3
Arrah	Rs. 3
Monghyr	Rs. 3

Nand Kishore Ram, a student of Second Year Class of Ranchi Intermediate College had received a monthly scholarship of Rs. 15 from David Scheme Fund, tenable for four years.

There were five girl schools and 113 day and night schools throughout the province where more than 3,000 Harijans received education. Besides the above, not less than 600 Harijans had been admitted into other schools through the efforts of the workers of our society. Over Rs. 500 worth of books and writing materials had been distributed out of the funds of our society. In all Rs. 2493-7-0 had been spent during the year under report for education of the Harijans.

In the province of Bihar, so far as education institutions are concerned, only Dom, Bhangi, Halkhor and Mehtars are considered as Depressed Classes. They are exempted from the payment of fees in all primary schools and had to pay reduced fee in higher schools. The government was considering the question of extending definition of Depressed Class to Harijans as enumerated in the Lothian Committee report. The Provincial Secretary addressed letters to the Chairmen of all Local Boards to extend the definition of Depressed Classes, as aforesaid, and are glad to record that the following bodies have passed resolutions extending the definitions: The District Boards of Muzaffarpur, Champaran, Chhapra, Arrah, Darbhanga, Patna, Monghyr, Purnea and Manbhum and the Municipalities of Muzaffarpur, Motihari, Bhagalpur and Lohardagga.

By virtue of the above, Harijans would be exempted from fees in all primary schools of the above-mentioned Local Bodies.

A Municipal Workers' Union had been formed at Purulia to redress the grievances and improve the condition of the Municipal employees. A bank has been started there for facilitating savings and to encourage thrift amongst the sweepers and protect them against extortionate moneylenders. A store has also been opened for supplying pure foodstuffs at moderate price. One Harijan is employed by Khadi Bhandar, Madhubani, district Darbhanga. The Saran Committee had given Rs. 15 to a Harijan youth for purchasing instruments of carpentry to start business.

292 visits were paid by Caste Hindus to Harijans'

quarters. Soap, soda and oil were distributed at numerous places.

168 meetings were held at which Harijans were exhorted to abstain from drinking and carrion eating. In several places Harijans took vow of abstinence.

There is very little difficulty about drawing water by Harijans from wells in the district of Ranchi, Manbhum, Hazaribagh, Santhal Parganas and Bhagalpur. In other places 646 wells were opened to Harijans.

Nine new wells had been opened for them. In the district of Monghyr, the Local Bodies had constructed 14 wells and sunk one pipe for Harijans.

Reports have reached us of 324 joint public meetings and 52 processions throughout the province. Many more are unreported.

One Harijan Municipal Commissioner was elected at each of the following places: Muzaffarpur, Hajipur and Chhapra. One Harijan had been nominated as Municipal Commissioner to Arrah Municipality by Government.

A Marbari gentleman of Ranchi had made a gift of two bighas of land for an orphanage and industrial home for Harijans. An ashram for Harijan workers had been opened at Gulzarbagh, Patna.

In Purulia, social religious meeting is held in different bastees (quarters) among the Harijans every evening in which kirtan and bhajan are sung and Ramayan and Mahabharat read. On every Purnima the kirtan parties of different basties gather together. Regular teams among the Harijans had been formed at Purulia and a competitive foot-ball play was held in which a silver shield and a medal were given.

The total receipts and expenditure for the Provincial Office were Rs. 6,518 and Rs. 5,988-0-6 respectively. The total receipts and expenditure for all the District Committees, excepting the District of Manbhum, have been Rs. 1,00,071-7-6 and Rs. 9,085-7-7 respectively.

The Municipal Board, Muzaffarpur, had passed the following resolution at a meeting held on 2nd February 1933:

"1. That the Dusadh, Chamar, Musahar, Dhobi, Mochi

and Pasi be added to the list of depressed classes as given in Bihar & Orissa Education Code.

2. That the teachers in all primary schools under the municipality be given a monthly allowance of anna one for every student of the depressed classes in Class I, provided that the number of such students was not less than four, annas two for every such student in Classes II and III and annas three in Class IV and V provided that the total amount of expenditure under this head did not exceed Rs. 300 a year for the present."[38]

Under the auspices of the S.U.S., a public meeting of Harijans and Caste Hindus was held at Choria (Ranchi) at which thirty-five Harijans signed pledge to take a bath daily, keep their quarter clean and to give up taking liquor and drugs and eating carrion.[39]

A well attended meeting of the Dhobis of Darbhanga was held under the auspices of the local District Committee and it was decided by them that they should abstain from toddy and liquor. Those violating their pledge, would have to pay a fine of Rs. 25 to the Panchayat.[40]

The Shri Siddheshwari Kali Temple in Deoghar was opened to the Harijans. The Shiva Temple of Royali (Behar), belonging to the Brahmin zamindar of the place, was thrown open to the Harijans. One each temple was opened in village Dumri, Sonbarsa, Shaharpur, Sursand, Harka Serai and the temple of Ram Ruplal Chaudhary, a prominent Mahajan of Mahanar Bazar, was opened to the Harijans. The Shiva Temple of Mohalla Begam (Arrah) was also opened. A primary school for Harijan children had been started in Deoghar. The Vidyalaya and Library of the Karmatanr Shri Nawagaur Pratisthan had been opened to the Harijans. The charitable dispensary of the Karmatanr Shri Nawagaur Pratisthan at Deoghar had been thrown open to the Harijan.[41]

One well at village Sonbarsa, one at village Shaharpur, a well belonging to Ram Ruplal Chaudhary of Mahanar Bazar, five wells at Chandan Patti, two wells belonging to

Ram Lakhan Singh of Fatehabad (Behar), wells in the villages of Raghunathpur and several in Bansi Pachra (Bihar). A well in the compound of M.E. School at Pupri Bazar, a well in village Harka, opened originally to Harijans but closed later on, had been re-opened. All wells in village Pariyapur, a well belonging to Ram Chalan Singh of village Bahighat also opened.[42]

On 24 June 1933, the proprietor Mahanth of Darshandasji had thrown open almost all his wells at his Deorhi at Maniar Chhapra Kaman and Madhaul, district Muzaffarpur, for the use of Harijans. Since 1921, there had been no obstruction to the use of his temples and wells by Harijans, but he had now made a public declaration of their being opened to Harijans also.[43]

Mukteshwar Ray Sharma, M.B.B.S., Maniari (district Muzaffarpur) had offered his services free to Harijans. A Harijan had been employed as a domestic servant by Mukteshwar Sharma, Asst. Surgeon, Maniari (Muzaffarpur).[44]

The Harijan Movement was progressing, guided by Mahatma Gandhi from the Yerveda Jail and later from outside, and it was engaging much attention of the national workers in Bihar as elsewhere. Mahatma Gandhi's guidance and advice were soon available to the relief organiser in Bihar. He had received information about the catastrophe through communique and reports in the newspapers and a telegram from Rajendra Prasad, dated 21 January 1934. Though he regarded this earthquake as a "Divine chastisement sent by God for our sins", particularly the "sin of untouchability", his heart was moved at the dissolution of "fair Bihar" and postponing his Harijan tour in the South, he started for Patna on 9 March 1934. "Whilst anti-untouchability work is undoubtedly greater and it is message of a permanent character", he expressed.

Mahatma Gandhi reached Patna in the evening of 11 March and stayed in the office of the Central Relief Committee. Accompanied by Rajendra Prasad, he went to Motihari and moved from place to place in the affected areas and comforting the distressed persons. Then he went to Chhapra and addressed there a mammoth meeting on 27 March asking the people to enable India to cast out the canker of untouchability.[47] On some date intervening 11 and 27 March 1934, Mahatma Gandhi had gone to Dinapur accompanied by Rajendra Prasad, and addressed there an audience of about 30,000 people on the Anathalaya grounds. He spoke on untouchability and relief work and made a special appeal to the students to come forward to help others in this disaster.[48] An address on behalf of the Dinapur citizens was presented to Mahatma Gandhi. Addressing the audience at Dinapur, Mahatma Gandhi said:

> "This is my second visit to Dinapur. In your address you have remarked that on account of the havoc caused by the recent earthquake the Harijan uplift movement had been thrown to the background. This is alright. Whatever I told you during the course of my speech at Patna, I will again say that almost everybody in this world has suffered and even then the public will soon forget this disaster caused by it. As we have completely forgotten the previous earthquakes in the history of this world, and consider them as historic incidents, we will hold the same view about this earthquake also after a due course of time. But so long as untouchability exists, we are reminded of our miseries. Some people consider untouchability as their religion, and if it disappears it would be a some sort of calamity to them. But if you look at it dispassionately, it cannot be defended. Those who call themselves *Sanatanists* understand that untouchability is indenfensible, and I think it is the staunchest class among *Sanatanists* who hold the view. After this earthquake we ought to be more humble as death is inevitable."[49]

At Sonepur Railway Station on 28 March 1934, Mahatma Gandhi said, "Yesterday, as the car was passing along the Gandak embankment, as I received a note from Doms of the village close by, telling me that they were suffering terribly from want of water, as the villagers would not allow them to take water from the common well. I drew the attention of the note and he promised me to put the thing right, if it was found that their complaints were justified. God's worth was felt equally by the rich and the poor, the Hindu and the Musalman, the castemen and the outcaste. Shall we not learn from God's terrible impartiality that it is criminal to consider any human being untouchable or lower than ourselves? If a single Dom or any other human being is denied use of the village wells, surely the lesson of the 15th January will have been cast upon us. I want to test you this very moment. I know you are all poor, earning bread by the sweat of your brows, but I know that there is in this vast crowd none so poor as not to be able to afford a pice. I want every one of you to contribute your coppers as a sign that you have repented of the sin of untouchability, that you do not consider any one lower than yourselves, and that is your own person you are determined to abolish all distinction of high and low, I do not want any of you to give me anything except on the condition I have made."[50]

From the railway station at Muzaffarpur, Mahatma Gandhi drove on a car straight to a meeting at Juran Chhapra, where he spoke on the efficacy of prayer for purifying the soul, and pleaded for the removal of untouchability, besides collecting funds.[51] He then proceeded to Darbhanga, where he made a touching appeal to the people for eradication of the sin of untouchability as a means of self-purification by drawing their attention to what he characterised as nature's signal. "Nature utters its warning to us", he said, "in a voice of thunder."[52]

At Bhagalpur, Mahatma Gandhi said as follows:

"The people of Bihpur brought money. I told them if only they believed untouchability to be a sin of Hindu society, they should subscribe for the funds I am raising. But they subscribed. Even the women caught hold of my feet to accept subscription. Purify yourselves. Untouchability is a social sin. Nobody is born untouchable. If you want to remove your distress, remove untouchability. No Viceroy's fund or the Central

> Committee can help you in this work. This is all that I had to say."[53]

When he re-entered the Patna district, the *Sanatanists* showed his black flags at Burhee. Speaking to them about toleration and mutual courtesy, he asked them to remember the famous saying of Tulsidas, "Kindness is the foundation of all religions, pride is the parent of all sins." Presiding over a meeting of the Central Relief Committee, Rajendra Prasad observed in a statement issued at this time, "Care should be taken to persuade the villagers to permit Harijans to take water from the same wells. But when this is impossible, Harijans should be provided with separate wells, preference in time being given to their wells."[54]

Mahatma Gandhi's tour in Bihar this time extended for more than two months and covered different parts of it. After visiting Assam from 18 April 1934, he came back to Patna on 24 April and recommended Harijan tour.

On 25 April, Mahatma Gandhi came by train to the Kulharia station and then went by motor car to Jamaria at the invitation of Radha Mohan Singh. From there he went to Arrah on a motor car and addressed a public meeting of about 10,000 persons, including some leaders at 9.15 A.M. on that day at the Raman Maidan. Some Harijan boys sang an opening song composed especially for the occasion, and garlanded him. Choudhary Sarafat Husain, Chairman of the Arrah Municipality, presented to him an Address, written on Khadi handkerchiefs in Hindi and Urdu on behalf of the local Municipal Commissioner, the English translation of which is as follows:

"Respected Mahatma Gandhijee, it is the day of the greatest pleasure today that the people of this town have got the opportunity of welcoming you in their midst. The people are overwhelmed with joy by seeing you today. We are unable to find words to express our pleasure. We pray to the Almighty Father to grant you longevity so that the people of the place may have the opportunity of seeing you occasionally.

"It is your real love and cult of Non-violence that has spread new light in the whole world. It is hoped that your principle will produce good results on the entire population. Mutual differences of opinion will disappear, and the foundation of goodwil and affection will be strong. You will be pleased to learn in this connection that our town is free from Hindu-Muslim tension, which, unfortunately, is found in other towns in this country.

"You will be pleased to learn that the members of the Chamar community of this town are more enlightened and educated than their fellow brethren elsewhere.

"Of the Harijan Pathshala in this town, we give grants-in-aid to two institutions.

"We regret to bring to your notice that our town has not escaped the devastation that has been wrought by the last earthquake in this province. Many houses have collapsed and deaths also have occured. There is not a single house in this town which has not been affected by the calamity. You had been touring for the uplift of depressed classes. It is worthy of you indeed. You have come here in this connection for which we are really overjoyed.

"Again, we cordially welcome you in our midst and pray to God to grant you long life."[55]

Radhika Raman Prasad Sinha of Surajpura, Chairman of the District Anti-Untouchability League, Bhagat Prasad and Shatrunjay Prasad Singh presented purses to him of the value of Rs. 500, Rs. 487 and Rs. 51 respectively. Some traders of the place and others also presented purses for Harijan work.[56]

While he halted for some time at the house of Bansropan Ram Choudhary leaving Arrah by 11'o clock train, Mahatma Gandhi came to Buxar in the midday of 25 April, where he halted for a few hours in the house of Jagdeva Roy, a local Pleader and Municipal Commissioner, before addressing a public meeting near the Fort at 4 P.M. Here also purse was presented to him for Harijan work. Both at Arrah and Buxar the *Sanatanists* tried to cause obstructions on the way and at the meetings and made demonstrations by showing black flags. But he proceeded undaunted on foot, unaccompanied by anybody, to the place of the meeting at Buxar.[57] Mahatma Gandhi's speech at Buxar was thus recorded in police report:

"President, brothers and sisters! I am thankful to you that all of you are sitting quiet. You know I am weak, but I shall try to speak loudly. You know that although being in such condition I did not feel any trouble in attending the meeting. If anybody fights I cannot control, rather I am injured by that. Atleast one of my brothers had a motor car push and I felt it very much.

"If any volunteer troubles any *Sanatanist*, in that case I would not be able to check myself. I know that *Sanatanist* would obstruct my motor car and I wouldnot like it and I would walk on foot. However, God would help me nobody knows. If any brother wishes to kill me, he cannot. I am sixty-five years old and there are several instances like that, but God saved me. Nobody can do anything to me. If any *Sanatanist*, who is here, even if he keeps my head in his arms, he cannot injure me.

"If I consider a thing to be a religious one, then how I can leave it!

"I also consider myself to be a *Sanatanist* and act according to my intellect which God has given to me. I have asked *Sanatanist* not to obstruct motor car or do any such act. My mission is that it is a sin to consider anybody low. God has created everybody in one kind.

"Tulsi Das observed himself to be low as well as several other saints observed like that. If anybody does not realise these things, it is not good for everybody who is known as human being. Harijan has also got privilege to go in the temple. I want to overhaul your thoughts and have explained the facts."

Starting from Buxar by the evening train on 25 April 1934, Mahatma Gandhi came to Jassidih where, also, on 26 April, the *Sanatanists* tried to cause obstructions, the rear pan of his car having been broken by them. After getting down from the car he walked a mile through the *Sanatanists.* There were anti-demonstrations at Deoghar. While regretting for the "manner of resistance", he appealed to the hearts and reason for the demonstrators.[58] He spent four busy days at Ranchi at the end of April and went to Orissa early in the next month.[59]

In view of the removal of the ban on the Congress organisation, the Working Committee Meeting at Wardha from 12 to 13 June 1934, advised responsible Congress workers to expedite the reorganisation of Congress Committees within their respective jurisdictions and engage Congressmen in constructive activities, such as, removal of untouchability and promotion of inter-communal unity.[60]

The Harijan Sewak Sangh, Hajipur, had been doing constructive work appreciably. Apart from visiting the Harijan quarters in the Hajipur town proper, the villages were also being visited. The needs of Harijans were ascertained. The psychology of the Harijan movement was being brought home to them. Besides, group meetings in several villages, in some of which women also participated, public meeting was held at Jamalpur in which speeches were delivered on the uplift of the Harijan. Uptil now, 16 villages had been visited by the prominent workers. In rural areas, Harijan schools had been opened in villages Belkunda, Baikunthpur, Dighi, Chak Bhoj, Belbarpur and Hajipur. 128 Harijan girls were receiving education at these schools.[61]

Principally through the efforts of Sarswati Devi, a prominent local worker, Harijan work was going on abreast there. She was to be congratulated on having opened schools for Harijan boys at Matwari, Mandu, Bishungarh and one near Ramgarh in the Hazaribagh district, where, in all, about 120 Harijan boys were getting instructions. Most of them had been provided with books and slates free of cost.[62]

Mahatmaji and his party attended a public meeting at Hazaribagh. Having thus concluded the function of the evening, Mahatmaji and his party left the place amidst defending cheers of "Mahatmaji ki Jai". Next morning he met the Harijan boys at the house of Sarswati Devi, where, after having distributed sweets to them, he, with his party, left for Gomio and Bermo.[63]

At Ranchi, the following address was presented to Mahatma Gandhi at the public meeting on May 3, 1934. The population of depressed classes in this district, as enumerated at the last Census, was about 82,000 when the society was started there in November 1932. The total number of children then in the primary schools of the whole district was only 919 in all. But thanks to Harijan Uplift Movement, we have at present day, besides a number of Harijan pupils in the Municipal, District Board and other schools, as many as 1,335 pupils in the 31 schools since started by our society. Two Harijan students had, through the society, received help for studies beyond the primary stage, one by award from the Raghu Mall Trust Fund of a stipend of Rs. 4 per month for high school education and another by the grant of a David Hare Scholarship of Rs. 15 per month, tenable for four years for college education.[64]

Mahatma Gandhi, in the course of his tour of Bihar, collected Rs. 23,742-10-4 for Harijan fund. The exact figure of collection from the district of Singhbhum was not available but the collection was reported to have exceeded Rs. 4,000.[65]

A meeting of the Hindus of Bakhari and its neighbouring villages was held at Bakhari on 9 May 1934 under the presidentship of Ram Charitra Singh, Chairman, District Board, Monghyr. A resolution appealing to the Hindus of the place to allow the Harijans to draw water from wells, educate their children in the same school and entrance into the temples and other public institution was adopted by an overwhelming majority in spite of the opposition of half a dozen people who had been deputed by some Mahanths.[66]

Considerable progress seemed to have been made in removal of illiteracy from the Harijans at Hajipur town. After organising a Harijan school under the auspices of the local theosophical society, the Harijan Sewak Sangh, Hajipur had so far been able to further establish eight such schools in the rural areas of this subdivision. The Sangh had supplied books, slates, copies, etc. to 104 students. Three students were recipient of special scholarship.[67]

The Hazaribagh District Harijan Sewak Sangh was busy preparing a scheme for the welfare work among the Harijans for which Mahatma Gandhi had toured round the country raising funds. The amount of money so raised in the district of Hazaribagh was Rs. 4000. After keeping one-fourth of it for central and provincial purpose, the entire amount of the balance would be spent in purely uplift work amongst the Harijans of the district. The District Committee had issued a circular to all the sub-committees to prepare a welfare scheme for their respective areas and submit the same to the District Office.[68]

It was reported that the opening ceremony of the Harijanpuri of the Marwari Relief Society was performed by Seth Jamna Lal Bajaj on 11 July 1934. Rajendra Prasad, M.M. Hafiz, Parvabati Devi and Ganesh Prasad, the President of Motihari Hindu Sabha also attended the function.[69]

Hazaribagh District Harijan Sewak Sangh celebrated the day when Mahatma Gandhi finished his All-India Harijan tour at Banaras on 29 July 1934. The workers of the Sangh went round the Harijan quarters looking to their cleanliness, pressing the inhabitants to give up the bad habits of drinking and eating carrion from 26 July 1934. Books, slates and clothes were then distributed to Harijan boys. Shakti Kant Bhattacharji, Advocate, announced a donation of Rs. 5 for the distribution of washing materials among Harijans.[70]

In pursuance of instruction from All-India Harijan Sewak Sangh, its branch at Hajipur organised the celebration of Harijan Day on 29 August 1934. The same celebration was also performed at Bhagalpur. A resolution was passed asking the Municipality of Bhagalpur to provide a water pipe and a latrine in a Mohalla Husainpur for the use of Harijans there.[71]

Harijan Sewak Sangh, Monghyr opened 24 Day Schools and 3 Night Schools, in which 700 Harijan students, including 50 girls were mostly Harijans. Expenditure to the tune of Rs. 1,316-12-0 was incurred for the maintenance of these institutions. Facilities were granted to 20 Harijan students for higher studies in middle and high schools by granting them a scholarship of Rs. 6-10 per month. The Sangh spent Rs. 145-7-6 for supplying books, slates, pencils, etc. and Rs. 135-3-9 for supplying clothes, etc., to the Harijan children. In all Rs. 264-4-6 were spent by the Sangh for the uplift of the Harijan in the year 1933.[72]

A Conference of the depressed classes of Monghyr was held on 28 December 1935, near Purab Sarai station in the Dharamshala of Dilip Narayan Singh under the presidentship of Ram Prasad, General Secretary, Bihar Provincial Depressed Classes League as it was formed under the name of "Monghyr Depressed Classes League."[73]

The second Harijan Sewak Conference was held on 15 January 1936 under the presidentship of Bindeshwari Prasad Verma, the Secretary of the Bihar Provincial Harijan Sewak Sangh, in Pandaul. Two resolutions, one requesting the District Sangh to observe a Harijan fortnight with a view to strengthen the Harijan work, and the other disapproving the policy of Ambedkar were passed.[74]

At Forbesganj, on 4 January 1936, Puran Dhobi performed "Satya Narayan Katha" with Pandit Padma Nath Dube as priest. It was attended by a good number of caste Hindus. The Panditji impressed upon the audience during his 'Katha' the crying need for reform in Hindu customs. The local Hindu Yuvak Sangh and Panditji were to be thanked for the first venture of this kind in this locality.[75]

The Harijans of Sitamarhi town were preparing for the performance of the "Satya Narayan Katha" in the newly built quarters constructed at the cost of government after the earthquake. A measure of relief to the Harijans had just been accomplished by the construction, by the Municipality, of a culvert to drain the water which used to accumulate in the Harijan quarters. Narsingha Prasad, Municipal Chairman, had taken personal interest in the matter. Another relief was rendered to the Harijans of Sitamarhi by sinking of a tube-well in the Harijan locality.[76]

Bhagalpur District Depressed Classes Conference was held at Bhagalpur in the Theosophical Society Hall on 23 February 1936 under the presidentship of Jag Jivan Ram, President, Bihar Provincial Depressed Classes League.[77]

A Subdivisional Conference of the Patna City depressed classes was held on 14 March 1937 at the Arya Samaj Mandir under the presidentship of Ram Prasad, C.T., M.L.A. The president, in course of his speech, advised the depressed classes for sending their children to the school.[78]

The Bihar Provincial Dusadh Mahasabha was held at Biharsharif on 29, 30 and 31 May under the presidentship of Sheonandan Lal of Monghyr. The president dealt with various evils prevailing among the Dusadh community and suggested the ways and means to remove them. The president, in course of his speech, laid much stress on the spread of education which he thought was the best remedy for the uplift of the community.[79]

He further pointed out that there was nothing to gain from changing the name of the Dusadh community to Gahlot Rajputs. Besides, if they declared themselves as Gahlot Rajput, hundreds of Dusadh students, who were getting help from the Harijan Sevak Sangh and other societies and had been granted free studentship in most of the government and government-aided schools, would be deprived of such help.[80]

The Monghyr Depressed Classes League at recent meeting held under the presidentship of R.N. Prasad, M.L A., passed a resolution expressing no confidence in the present ministry in Bihar and requesting the immediate summoning of the legislature. By another resolution the League requested the government to increase depressed classes' representation in Local Bodies.[81]

Syed Mahmood, Minister of Education, reached Bettiah. Referring to the Harijans' address, he assured them that he would see that the government orders were strictly carried out if not done so far. He mentioned that a sum of Rs. 36,000 was allotted in this year's budget for granting scholarship to the deserving Harijan students.[82]

District officials had been asked to pay special attention to the claims of Harijans in appointing chaprasies and menials by Bihar ministry.[83]

The Doranda Notified Area Committee has started a school meant exclusively for the children of the Harijan and depressod class employees of the Committee. The Committee had about five other general schools, which had no restriction against Harijan and depressed class boys. Education was free in the primary classes.[84]

The following press note had been issued by the Government of Bihar :

> "Out of the funds sanctioned by the government for the award of special scholarship to Harijan boys for technical and industrial training in and outside the province, the following scholarships are hereby awarded :
>
> (1) One scholarship of Rs. 20 a month to Ram Autar Ram for practical training at the Tata Iron and Steel Company Ltd., Jamshedpur, for one year with effect from the 1st August 1938.
>
> (2) One scholarship of Rs. 20 a month to Guru Das for training in subordinate Civil Engineering course at the Bihar College of Engineering, Patna for a period of two years.
>
> (3) One scholarship of Rs. 7 per month to Mahavir Lal for training in tailoring at Technical Institute, Monghyr for one year."[85]

Muzaffarpur celebrated the first day of Harijan Week on 24 September 1938 in a befitting manner. All the Harijan and non-Harijan students participated. Sports were organised.[86]

At a meeting of the Harijans of Gaya District convened by Bachha Singh, a Commissioner of the Local Municipal Board, held at the local Balak Sudhar Pathshala on 25th instant under the chairmanship of Jangi Singh, Harijan Sangh, was formed with Bachha Singh as its president. It was also resolved that proper training should be imparted to the Harijan women for doing the work of midwifery.[87]

Jaglal Chaudhary came to Jamshedpur to attend the opening ceremony of the new Harijan school at Dalkadih. While opening the school he paid a high tribute to the Tata

Iron and Steel Company in general and M.J.J. Ghandy, the General Manager of the Company in particular, paying for so much attention to the cause of Harijans at Jamshedpur and spending a considerable amount for their uplift.[88]

Fatwa Thana Ravidas Conference was held on 30 November 1938. Jagjivan Ram enumerated the various complaints which the members of the community made to him in the meeting. He advised them to organise themselves together with all community which were being oppressed and suppressed by the privileged classes and to learn to protest against 'Begari' and illegal exaction.[89]

Under the auspices of the Bihar Theosophical Federation, efforts were being made to open an industrial school from 1 August 1939, in which training in leather work, *durry* making, weaving, etc. was given to the Harijan students free of charge. In selection of candidate for admission to the school preference was given to the Harijan students. It is understood that 40 students would be admitted in the first instance, students for admission must be over 12. The institution would be managed by the Bihar Theosophical Federation and would be aided by the government of Bihar.[90]

The mass literacy work in Siwan sub-division was being conducted by Baijnath Prasad, Headmaster, D.A.V. School and Chairman of the Siwan Municipal Board. He contributed much towards the furtherance of the literacy campaign to pay special attention to the education of the Harijans.[91]

The General Secretary, Bihar Provincial Congress Committee directed to all the District Congress Committees: "The members of the depressed classes have also been elected and nominated in various District Boards of the Province. It was fair and legitimate that they should receive encouragement at the time of election of executive in the District Boards. It was an open secret that they could not get any position unless and until they were favourably treated and given a chance to rise. We were in duty bound to look to their welfare at least in political life and, as such, he would appeal to us not to forget them at the right moment when the elections of Chairman and Vice-Chairman for local bodies took place.[92]

Bindeshwari Prasad Verma, M.L.A., Secretary, Harijan Sewak Sangh, proposed to celebrate the completion of Thakkar Bapa's 70th year by presenting him with a purse of Rs. 70,000 for the Harijan cause. Mahatma Gandhi and Rajendra Prasad had already issued appeals to all to subscribe liberally to this fund.[93]

Perhaps for the first time in the annals of this province, a Harijan had been elected Chairman of the Buxar Local Board.[94]

During the period under review, Bihar's response to the call of Mahatma Gandhi for the removal of the curse of untouchability was splendid. Here work for the upliftment of the Harijans or the depressed classes as the Mahatma called them, progressed satisfactorily. Efforts made for the opening of temples to them were successful at several places. Persistent efforts of the leaders bore fruits. Consequently children of the untouchables were admitted into schools. They were getting access to wells and a number of men were ceasing to have any objection to water and even food being touched by them. Thus, in Bihar, there was some relaxation in the rigour of untouchability.

References

1. *1921 Movement : Reminiscence*, forwarded by V.V. Giri, p. 195.
2. *The Non-Cooperation and Khilafat Movement in Bihar and Orissa*, p. 92.
3. Prasad, Rajendra : *Atmakatha*, p. 213.
4. Datta, K.K. : *History of the Freedom Movement in Bihar*, Vol. I, p. 453.
5. *The Searchlight*, January 9, 1924.
6. Datta, K.K. : *History of the Freedom Movement in Bihar*, Vol. I, p. 460.
7. *The Searchlight*, April 11, 1924.
8. *Young India*, pp. 57-58.
9. Ibid., 1927-28, pp. 65-67.
10. *Bihar Provincial Congress Committee's Report*, 1928-29.
11. Ibid.
12. Ibid.
13. Ibid.

14. *The Searchlight*, January 22, 1930.
15. Nehru, Jawahar Lal : *Autobiography*, p. 210.
16. *The Searchlight*, June 16, 1931.
17. Ibid., October 10, 1931.
18. *Weekly report of the Superintendent of Police*, Shahabad, October 23, 1931.
19. *The Searchlight*, December 13, 1931.
20. *The Indian Nation*, January 4, 1932.
21. Quoted in Tendulkar, *Mahatma*, Vol. III, p. 217.
22. *The Indian Nation*, April 18, 1932.
23. Ibid., April 20, 1932.
24. Ibid , April 25, 1932.
25. Datta, K.K. : *History of the Freedom Movement in Bihar*, Vol. II, p. 194
26. *Fortnightly report of the Patna Commissioner* for the period ending July 27, 1932.
27. *Letter from the Patna Commissioner to the Chief Secretary*, September 26, 1932.
28. Ibid.
29 Ibid.
30. Ibid.
31. *Weekly report of the Collector of Shahabad to the Commissioner*, September 30, 1932.
32 *Fortnightly report of the Patna Commissioner* for the period ending October 13, 1932 and October 27, 1932. At this time some students of Patna College ate with sweepers.
33. Datta, K.K. : *History of the Freedom Movement in Bihar*, Vol. II, p. 196.
34. It is mentioned in *Contemporary Government Report* that at this meeting 1200 persons were present including about 20 ladies and 10 children.
35. *Letter from the Chief Secretary to the Commissioner of Bhagalpur*, February 2, 1933. Babu Sridhar Samal, a Sub-Inspector of Schools was refused permission to join it. C.F.—"Anti-Untouchability is a social movement, but the margin between it and connected political movement is, at present, vagary. Public servant should regard this movement as one of the controversial and political character with which they should not be associated." D.O. from the Commissioner of Bhagalpur to the District Magistrate, Monghyr, Jan. 25, 1933.
36. *Report of the Secretary, Provincial Board of Anti-Untouchability League*. Quoted in Datta, K.K.'s *History of the Freedom Movement in Bihar*, Vol. II, pp. 197-201.
37. *Fortnightly report of the Patna Commissioner* for the period ending November 22, 1933.
38. *Harijan*, February 25, 1933.

39. Ibid., April 8, 1933.
40. Ibid , April 29, 1933.
41. Ibid., May 13, 1933.
42. Ibid., July 8, 1933.
43. Ibid.
44. Ibid.
45. Poet Tagore gave a short *rejoinder* to this statement. Agreeing with the poet, Nehru considered it to be a "staggering remark." Autobiography, p. 490.
46. Tendulkar, *Mahatma*, Vol. II, p. 309.
47. Quoted in Tendulkar, *Mahatma*, Vol. III, p. 313.
48. Ibid.
49. Ibid.
50. Quoted in Tendulkar, *Mahatma*, Vol. III, pp. 313-314.
51. *The Indian Nation*, April 3, 1934.
52. Quoted in Tendulkar, *Mahatma*, Vol. III, p. 315.
53. *The Indian Nation*, April 6 1934.
54. Ibid., April 8, 1934.
55. For Hindi version of it vide *Appendix X-XV*, K.K. Datta, Vol. II.
56. *Letter from the District Magistrate, Shahabad to the Chief Secretary, Bihar and Orissa*, April 38, 1934.
57. Singh, Anugraha Narayan: *Mere Sansmaran*, p. 152.
58. *The Indian Nation*, April 27, 1934.
59. Ibid , May 2, 1934.
60. Datta, K K. : *History of the Freedom Movement in Bihar*, Vol. II, p. 230.
61. *The Indian Nation*, April 11, 1934.
62. Ibid.
63. Ibid , May 4, 1934.
64. Ibid.
65. Ibid. May 9, 1934.
66. Ibid , May 15, 1934.
67. Ibid., June 22, 1934.
68. Ibid., July 5, 1934.
69. Ibid., July 18, 1934.
70. Ibid., July 31, 1934.
71. *Harijan*, September 2, 1934.
72. *The Indian Nation*, September 25, 1934.
73. Ibid., January 4, 1935.
74. *Harijan*, January 16, 1936.
75. Ibid.
76. *The Indian Nation*, January 20, 1936.
77. Ibid., February 29, 1936.
78. Ibid., March 18, 1937.
79. *Fortnightly report of the Patna Commissioner* for the period ending May 31, 1937.

80. Ibid.
81. *The Indian Nation*, June 20, 1937.
82. Ibid , October 21, 1937.
83. Ibid , November 18, 1937.
84. Ibid., August 5, 1938.
85. *The Indian Nation*, August 14, 1938.
86. Ibid., September 29, 1938.
87. *Fortnightly report of the Commer.* for period ending Sept. 30, 1938.
88. *The Indian Nation*, October 14, 1938.
89. Ibid , December 4, 1938.
90. *Harijan*, July 31, 1939.
91. *The Indian Nation*, September 2, 1939.
92. Ibid., October 14, 1939.
93. *Harijan*, November 17, 1939.
94. *The Indian Nation*, December 21, 1939.

Conclusion

The post-first World War period witnessed events of extra-ordinary importance in the history of Indian National movement. Among other significant events, the emergence of Gandhi on the political horizon of India brought about a radical transformation in the arena of Indian politics as well as socio-economic life of the people. Gandhi was an ardent champion of truth and non-violence, and armed with these two new, bold and exemplary weapons of arousing mass consciousness, he plunged himself successfully in the Champaran movement in 1917. These gospels, when experimented, proved to be a veritable nursery of India's emerging nationalism and most efficient means of realising the noble cause of the socio-economic and political salvation of the masses from the accumulated anomalies.

The year 1920 marked a new phase in the history of the struggle for freedom and under the leadership of Mahatma Gandhi the Indian National Congress launched a severe attack on the economic policy of the British Government in India by inaugurating a series of constructive programmes and initiating new steps in the life of common people. The resolution passed and endorsed by the Calcutta and Nagpur sessions of the Congress respectively heralded the dawn of a new economic consciousness among the people in general and the Congress workers in particular with regard to the production and use of khadi and boycott of foreign goods in India.

The Bihar delegates attending the Nagpur session of 1920 returned with a new spirit. The gospel of 'swadeshi' was preached by them among the masses with great zeal. Promptly and enthusiastically Bihar responded to the resolutions of the Bezwada Congress held in April 1921 and set herself to the task of fulfilling the condition of having and setting up 2 lakhs of charkha in good order. Forty-eight depots were opened in the eleven districts of the province, so that the people could get raw cotton and charkhas without any difficulty. At several places in Bihar the constructive programmes as laid down by the Bardoli resolution, were tackled with right earnest.

The Provincial Congress Committee presided over by Maulana Mazharul Haque, formed a Provincial Khaddar Board with a view to making efforts for popularising the cult of khaddar. Rajendra Prasad inaugurating the all-India Swadeshi exhibition at the Belgaum Congress on 23 December 1924, expressed his opinion that khaddar should form an important place in the national life of the people. He emphasised that if the people devoted themselves to the cause of charkha and khaddar, it would successfully effect a complete boycott of foreign goods in Bihar and also in the country as a whole. Rajendra Prasad took the initiative of starting the All-India Spinners' Association, which subsequently became an integral part of the Congress organisation. Thus under Rajendra Prasad's guidance the work of khadi progressed both qualitatively and quantitatively. Further, to popularise the use of khadi, exhibitions were held at different places in Bihar in 1926 and 1927 under the able guidance of Rajendra Prasad, who was a true disciple of Gandhi. Subsequently, exhibitions were organised at Arrah, Muzaffarpur, Mairva, Gaya, Giridih, Patna, Motihari, Bettiah, Jamshedpur, Laheriasarai, Deoghar, Hazaribagh, Ranchi. During the last days of his tour in 1927, Gandhiji met the khadi workers of Bihar and on this occasion a special khadi exhibition was organised by Rajendra Prasad in the Sinha Institute of Patna. There had been a tremendous rush at the exhibition and "Congressmen and non-Congressmen, Government officials, zamindars, lawyers, big and small merchants and in more cases even Europeans visited the exhibition."

The khadi work continued in Bihar with a sense of

dedication under the leadership of Rajendra Prasad. Besides him, there were several other important persons, such as, Girish Tewary, Ram Charan Singh, Janakdhari Prasad, Lakshmi Narayan, Deo Narayan Lal, Jaglal Chaudhary, Latifur Rahman, Braj Kishore Prasad, Ram Narayan, Ramanand and others, who exerted their endeavours in popularising the use of khadi throughout the province of Bihar.

The Bihar Youth Conference, the Bihari Students' Conference, Bihar Seva Sangh, Bihar Branch of the All-India Spinners' Association, Mahila Sabha, Gandhi Ashram, Gandhi Kutir, Charkha Sangh and cooperative societies contributed remarkably in popularising the use of khadi among the people of Bihar. Thus the charkha was adopted as subsidiary industry to supplement the meagre income of the vast body of poor agricultural population and symbolised the model of India's old economy which was marked by a fair coordination between agriculture and industry conducive to the economic welfare of the country as a whole.

Reform of the educational system was another significant aspect of Gandhiji's constructive programme. The system of education as it then existed, was imposed upon the nation by the alien government to serve the own administrative and imperialistic requirements. Gandhiji, therefore, started a new national scheme of education with the aim of preparing the students for the good of the country and enabling them to earn their livelihood through instruction of practical nature. Hence the scheme was not entirely new. Even in the swadeshi days this formed an important part of the swadeshi programme. It was again tackled by the Home Rule Movement under Annie Besant. All these schemes of educational reforms were to give preference to the mother tongue instead of the foreign language, English, which was introduced as the medium of instruction.

Another very remarkable aspect of Gandhiji's scheme of education was to make education relevant in the socio-economic set up of an individual's life as well as the life of the nation. To Gandhiji, education should be of some utility and value. He, therefore, correlated education with activity. Popular political education was of utmost importance in India, as it would keep the people informed of their rights and obligations and prepare them during India's struggle for freedom. The charkha had an important place in national scheme of education, as "it is a science which gives us a knowledge of the means of ameliorating the condition of the masses."

It was under the influence of Gandhiji's ideals that some national schools were started here and some existing ones were nationalised by repudiating the affiliation to the university. Gandhi gave this province much needed impetus by placing at her disposal seven or eight thousand rupees, then collected in Bihar, for the purpose of establishing national educational institutions. As a result, several national schools were started and on 6 February 1921 Gandhi himself performed the opening ceremony of the National College and of the Bihar Vidyapith. The Bihar Vidyapith was to "co-ordinate the activities of all the national institutions that were springing up in the province and to control and guide them. In all the institutions the medium of instruction was Hindi. Spinning was compulsory and weaving was also taught in some of them.

With the opening of the Bihar Vidyapith, a number of national educational institutions sprang up in different parts of Bihar. A few schools had been closed later due to paucity of funds, and even the Bihar Vidyapith faced financial stringencies. Rajendra Prasad who deeply involved himself in the constructive programmes of Gandhiji, made sincere efforts to improve the financial condition by raising subscriptions from the people To make the Vidyapith attractive to the students, some eminent scholars from outside Bihar were invited to join its staff. Another significant event as regards the establishment of national institutions in Bihar, was establishment of the Bihar Mahila Vidyapith on 4 July 1934. Its aim was to arrange "for the imparting of education which would train up the daughters of Bihar into useful and cultured women, heads of happy household. light of the home." Hence, the people of Bihar played a commendable role in replacing the alien system of education by the National Scheme of Education. In spite of several handicaps, missionary zeal of our leaders and people resulted in the establishment of several national educational institutions imparting education to keep the people informed of their rights and obligations and prepare them for India's struggle for freedom.

The organisation of local arbitration courts or Panchayats was an integral part of Gandhi's constructive programmes. Bihar witnessed events of extra-ordinary importance as far as the establishment of popular assemblies was concerned. The Nagpur Congress gave a fillip to such events. Gandhi was a source of great inspiration to the workers and delegates who attended the Congress session. The Delegates of Bihar returned to their respective areas of activities with a passionate zeal and soon pre-occupied themselves with the tasks of establishing local Panchayats. This constructive programme of Gandhiji made rapid progress in the different parts of Bihar in the early months of 1921. The work of the organisation of local arbitration courts or Panchayats continued throughout the period. It was all due to the personal attention of Rajendra Prasad and Mazharul Haque that the people took active interest, and Panchayats had been established in a large number of villages in the districts of Saran, Muzaffarpur, Shahabad Darbhanga, Patna, Gaya, Champaran, Bhagalpur, Hazaribagh, Ranchi, Palamu and Monghyr.

In these panchayats there were Rashtriya Judge, Rashtriya Collector and Magistrate to try civil and criminal cases. The panchayats, besides these public officers, had a very thorough organisation of volunteers who impressed upon the villagers to lodge their complaints or cases in the panchayats and boycott Government ccurts. The work of these panchayats was either to arbitrate or to take positive action in establishing a compromise between the contending parties. The appeal against the decision of the local courts could be made to a body called Halka Panchayat consisting of the representatives of ten to fifteen villages. From the Halka Panchayat a case might go up to the final Panchayat Board, consisting of five honest and influential men nominated by the Thana Congress Committee. Popular enthusiasm about the village panchayats was so high that at times people resorted to social boycott with a view to enforcing the decision of such panchayats. By making the working of the village panchayats a success, the people of Bihar remained in the vanguard of the movement of Gandhiji which aimed at eroding the base of the British administration in India by paths of truth and non-violence.

The Nagpur Session of the Indian National Congress (1920) really proved to be an extraordinary important session. There was by this time a profound awakening in Bihar, and a large number of Bihar delegates returned from there with a sense of a new spirit. It found expression in the varied activities consistent with the changed programmes and principles of the Congress. The volunteers began to be recruited in the different parts of Bihar. The Bihar Provincial Congress Committee issued general instruction to the workers to pay attention more and more to the work of organisation than delivering speeches. Subsequently, in the meeting of the All India Congress Committee, held at Bezwada on 31 March and 1 April 1921, a resolution was passed with a view of raising the fund of All-India Tilak Swaraj Fund to one crore of rupees and enrolling the Congress register one crore of Congress members on or before 30 June. The province of Bihar was to raise 10 lakhs of rupees and enrol 10 lakhs of members in the Congress register. Bihar promptly set herself to the task of fulfilling these conditions during the Satyagraha Week commencing from 6 April 1921. In spite of various handicaps, Bihar collected Rs. 7.5 lakhs for Tilak Swaraj Fund and enrolled large number of members. Further, by the end of June, the Congress organisation was consolidated here which "stood the test of the time and government repression."

In response to the instruction of the Working Committee of the All-India Congress Committee held at Bombay on 3 November 1921, the Bihar Congress Committee formed the Bihar Volunteer Corps to carry out the national scheme of programme. The popular enthusiasm for the cause of nationalism increased tremendously and the recruitment of volunteers showed a promising figure. The people contributed liberally to the Tilak Swaraj Fund also. Gandhi's Bihar tours in 1925 and 1927 gave additional impetus to the consolidation work. In meetings addressed by him in the different parts of

Bihar, such as, Purulia, Kusumpur, Ranchi, Deoghar, Hajipur, Mairva, Gaya, Dalsingsarai, Samastipur and Darbhanga, etc., he made appeals for enrolment of Congress members and contribution to the Congress Fund. The people responded to his call by enlisting themselves as members of the Congress and strengthening the Congress organisation by donating liberally to its fund. The collection of funds and enrolment of volunteers continued throughout the following years. The branches of the Gandhi Seva Sangh, the Bihar Provincial Conciliatory Board and Hindustani Seva Dal also contributed a lot in organising the volunteers corps of the Congress. It was due to the consolidation of the Congress organisation that Bihar enthusiastically responded to the national call of "Simon Go Back" and the civil disobedience movement. As a result the Congress won the election of 1937 and formed the popular ministry in Bihar.

Further, restraining the pernicious effects of the communal frenzy was also an important item in Gandhiji's constructive programmes in Bihar. The canker of communalism polluted the whole atmosphere and on account of this evil there occurred bloodsheds in several places. The most serious communal riot took place at Calcutta, which had repercussions in Bihar. Minor communal clashes broke out at Sasaram, Monghyr, Gaya, Bhagalpur, Darbhanga and Muzaffarpur, and many people perished in the communal frenzy. The situation in Bihar, however, became distinctly better and in 1926 the Bakr-Id festival passed off without any grave disorder. These riots led to the establishment of Conciliation Committees and unity conference whose sole tasks were to maintain communal harmony and amity between the two communities. Mazharul Haque took the lead in organising a conference at Chhapra on 10 June 1926 of prominent Congressmen of Bihar, members of the Khilafat Committee, and several others outside these two organisations. After discussion, the members expressed their determination to take adequate steps for checking the evils of communalism. Mazharul Haque, Maulana Muhammad Safi, Jagat Narayan Lal, Anugraha Narayan Sinha, Rajendra Prasad, Saiyid Sulaiman Naqvi, Abdul Bari, Srikrishna Sinha and several others moved in the different parts of Bihar, addressed meetings, making fervent appeals laying considerable emphasis on the need of maintaining communal unity and harmony. As a result, the atmosphere in Bihar remained comparatively free from the injurious effects of the communal riots.

Further, the Gandhi Seva Sangh was organised in Bihar to push forward the constructive activities of the Congress. It particularly pleaded for communal harmony, which took the form of inculcating in all hearts and minds love for Hindu-Muslim unity.

The Bihar tours of Mahatma Gandhi during the period of our study proved fruitful as far as the promotion of Hindu-Muslim unity was concerned. His addresses and appeals at the different meetings proved effective in stemming the tide of communal tension. It may be noted in this respect that Maulana Abul Kalam Azad's visit to Patna in 1930 had produced a salutary effect on the people of Bihar. Many youths of the Muslim community started an organisation under the presidentship of Abdul Bari with the object of popularising the idea of independence in their community. However, towards the end of the period of our study, for some reason or other, passion occasionally rose high and there were communal frictions, mostly of minor nature, here and there. The communal concord established in the early period was marred under certain foreign forces. The outlook of the Muslim League had become anti-Congress and its influence had gradually increased in Bihar. The League continued to make progress and a large number of Muslims joined it. Numerous meetings were held in Bihar and Jinnah himself visited Bihar for propagating the ideals of the League. These gave impetus to the influence of the League and in Bihar, subsequently, some stray cases of communal disturbances had been reported in several parts of Bihar.

But good results sometimes come out of evil. The bitterness of the communal outbreaks in Bihar produced a change of outlook towards the end of August 1938, particularly among the leaders of the League. With the object of establishing peace, Conciliation Peace Brigades were formed at several places and even stage performances were organised by the two communities with a view to promoting communal harmony. It was due to the untiring efforts of the leaders of Bihar, who moved from place to place for preaching sanity among the people of both the communities, and organised committees, conferences, organisations working for communal harmony, that Bihar remained comparatively free from severe communal riots. The people of Bihar, henceforward upheld the verdict of Gandhiji that Hindu-Muslim unity was vital for the struggle of freedom.

Untouchability was another curse of Indian society, which Gandhiji wanted to remove through his constructive programmes. According to Gandhiji, "untouchability is a cruel and inhuman institution. It violates human dignity. It deadens sensibility of both the oppressor and the oppressed. Untouchability is against the spirit of democracy, which makes no distinction among citizens. Further, Gandhiji said that the untouchables were the poorest sections of the Indian society and their avenues of employment were strictly limited. They lived apart in unhygienic surroundings on the outskirts of villages and cities. Though they were Hindus and believed and worshipped Hindu gods and goddesses, they were not allowed to enter the Hindu temples, institutions like schools, hostels and hotels were closed to them. Gandhiji asserted "that religion and nation would be blotted out from the face of the earth which pinned faith to injustice, untruth or violence." Gandhiji's concern for the untouchables and down-trodden was evident from his addresses during his tours in Bihar for popularising his constructive programmes. He laid special stress on the amelioration of the untouchables and the removal of untouchability. The Indian National Congress issued instructions to its leaders and workers in this connection.

The response of the people of Bihar in this respect was splendid. The work of the upliftment of the depressed classes or the Harijans, as Mahatma Gandhi called them, had begun with the Ahmedabad Congress in 1920. Since then several meetings were held throughout the province attended by the caste Hindus and depressed classes. In such meetings appeals were made the leaders to open the temples to Harijans or depressed classes. It had been very successful at several places. Children of the so-called untouchables began to be admitted to the schools, wells were made accessible to them and inter-caste dinners were well attended by the people of all castes. The role of organisations like Gandhi Seva Sangh, Bihar Students' Conference, Harijan Sevak Sangh, Provincial Board of Anti-Untouchability League and Bihar Provincial Depressed League had been commendable in this respect. Untouchability abolition weeks were observed with the aim of educating the people for discarding this practice. The organisers of such weeks tried to impress upon the upper caste Hindus that untouchables should not be looked down upon and the physical contact with them should not be considered objectionable.

Such attempts of eradicating the social evil of untouchability had received impetus by the tours of Gandhiji in Bihar. Gandhiji received purses and contributions during his Harijan tours in Bihar, and such purses were spent on opening schools, supplying books, slates and copies to Harijan boys and girls. Educational stipends and scholarships were also given to the Harijan students. Besides him, Amrit Lal V. Thakkar, Rajendra Prasad, Raja Radhika Raman Prasad Sinha and other leaders exhorted the high caste Hindus to treat the so-called untouchables properly and respectfully and to afford to them all facilities for their social and educational uplift. As a result of the persistent efforts of the local and national leaders and various other organisations working for the uplift of the untouchables, Bihar witnessed unprecedented relaxation in the rigours of untouchability.

The constructive programmes of the Gandhian era, which formed an important part in the history of India's national struggle for freedom, had its root in the fateful soil of Bihar. The Champaran Satyagraha of Gandhiji reared a crop of leaders in Bihar, who threw themselves heart and soul into the lap of Gandhiji, who had inaugurated a series of constructive programmes through which India and her people could attain salvation and nationhood. These enthusiastic and patriotic leaders of Bihar followed the path dictated by

Gandhiji. Step by step the national feeling of the people was aroused and they were awaken from the deep slumber of social, economic and political evils. It was significant that the spirit generated by Gandhiji among the people of Bihar led to the successful completion of the non-cooperation and civil disobedience movements, besides a host of other constructive programmes associated with them. The politics of Swaraj with all its social, economic and political goals had not only put the nation on the threshold of freedom but also put Bihar in the forefront of India's struggle for freedom.

APPENDICES

APPENDIX I

REPORT ON NATIONAL SCHOOLS

For the Half Year ending December 1922

Sl. No.	District	As on July 1922 Schools	Pupils	As on Jan. 1, 1923 Schools	Pupils
1.	Patna	34	1453	21	972
2.	Gaya	26	963	14	932
3.	Shahabad	25	959	11	255
4.	Saran	85	3110	52	1502
5.	Champaran	100	3366	66	2308
6.	Muzaffarpur	46	1632	44	1478
7.	Darbhanga	27	1388	18	1052
8.	Monghyr	66	1980	31	1200
9.	Bhagalpur	38	1140	24	854
10.	Purnea	31	930	14	386
11.	Santhal Parganas	3	90	2	149
12.	Hazaribagh	10	342	1	82
13.	Ranchi	1	40	1	50
14.	Palamu	10	252	6	127
15.	Manbhum	5	380	4	369
16.	Singhbhum	2	140	3	141
	Total	509	18,155	312	11,867

For the Half Year ending 30th June 1923

Sl. No.	District	As on			
		Jan. 1, 1923		July 1, 1923	
		Schools	Pupils	Schools	Pupils
1.	Patna	21	972	18	907
2.	Gaya	14	932	13	433
3.	Saran	52	1502	48	1492
4.	Shahabad	11	265	5	105
5.	Champaran	66	2308	50	1644
6.	Muzaffarpur	44	1478	30	1022
7.	Darbhanga	18	1052	16	1028
8.	Monghyr	31	1200	18	925
9.	Bhagalpur	24	854	12	371
10.	Purnea	14	386	13	439
11.	Santhal Parganas	2	149	4	196
12.	Hazaribagh	1	82	1	31
13.	Ranchi	1	50	1	25
14.	Palamu	6	127	3	105
15.	Manbhum	4	369	3	245
16.	Singhbhum	3	141	3	155
	Total	312	11,867	238	9,112

Ref. : Political Special File No. 52/1923.

For the Half Year ending 31 July 1923

Sl. No.	District	As on July 1, 1923 Schools	Pupils	As on January 1, 1924 Schools	Pupils
1.	Patna	18	907	17	757
2.	Gaya	13	433	10	314
3.	Shahabad	5	105	3	50
4.	Saran	48	1492	33	1055
5.	Champaran	50	1644	47	1740
6.	Muzaffarpur	30	1022	22	648
7.	Darbhanga	16	1028	12	625
8.	Monghyr	18	925	15	783
9.	Bhagalpur	12	371	13	473
10.	Purnea	13	439	8	258
11.	Santhal Parganas	4	196	2	119
12.	Hazaribagh	1	31	1	30
13.	Ranchi	1	25	1	35
14.	Palamu	3	105	Nil	Nil
15.	Manbhum	3	245	3	170
16.	Singhbhum	3	155	3	95
	Total	238	9,123	190	7,152

For the Half Year ending 30 June 1924

Sl. No.	District	As on Jan. 1, 1924 Schools	Pupils	July 1, 1929 Schools	Pupils
1.	Patna	17	757	15	748
2.	Gaya	10	314	9	241
3.	Shahabad	3	50	8	178
4.	Saran	33	1055	26	1069
5.	Champaran	47	1740	44	1522
6.	Muzaffarpur	22	648	19	486
7.	Darbhanga	12	625	8	479
8.	Monghyr	15	783	15	703
9.	Bhagalpur	13	473	13	627
10.	Purnea	8	258	8	258
11.	Santhal Parganas	2	119	3	168
12.	Hazaribagh	1	30	2	77
13.	Ranchi	1	35	1	36
14.	Palamu	Nil	—	Nil	—
15.	Manbhum	3	170	3	158
16.	Singhbhum	3	95	3	135
	Total	196	7,152	177	6,885

Ref. : Political Special File No. 79/1924.

For the Half Year ending December 31, 1928

Sl. No.	District	As on 1st July 1928 Schools	Pupils	1st January, 1929 Schools	Pupils
1.	Patna	4	351	4	295
2.	Gaya	—	—	—	—
3.	Shahabad	2	97	2	74
4.	Saran	2	87	2	91
5.	Champaran	4	333	4	338
6.	Muzaffarpur	2	90	2	123
7.	Darbhanga	6	324	6	279
8.	Monghyr	6	321	6	276
9.	Bhagalpur	1	60	1	120
10.	Purnea	3	100	3	78
11.	Santhal Parganas	1	62	1	62
12.	Hazaribagh	—	—	—	—
13.	Ranchi	—	—	—	—
14.	Palamu	—	—	—	—
15.	Manbhum	—	—	—	—
16.	Singhbhum	—	—	—	—
	Total	31	1825	31	1656

For the Half Year ending June 1929

1.	Patna	4	295	3	253
2.	Gaya	...	—	—	—
3.	Shahabad	2	74	2	102
4.	Saran	2	91	2	95
5.	Champaran	4	338	4	275
6.	Muzaffarpur	2	123	2	105
7.	Darbhanga	6	229	6	223
8.	Monghyr	6	276	6	256
9.	Bhagalpur	1	120	1	120
10.	Purnea	3	78	2	65
11	Santhal Parganas	1	62	1	62
12.	Ranchi	—	—	—	—
13.	Hazaribagh	—	—	—	—
14.	Palamu	—	—	—	—
15.	Manbhum	—	—	—	—
16.	Singhbhum	—	—	1	127
	Total	31	1656	30	1486

Ref. : Political Special File No. 55/1929, Bihar State Archives, Patna.

The report for the six months ending 31 December 1928 shows no change in the number of schools but the number of pupils had decreased by about 6.5%, the total number now being nearly the same as a year ago though the figure soared 8% in the 1st half of 1928.

The decrease was most noticeable in Darbhanga, Patna and Monghyr, while Bhagalpur has had a cent per cent rise and Muzaffarpur nearly 37%.

The number of schools had fallen to 31—Patna and Bhagalpur losing one each.

The pupils had decreased by about 6%. The decrease was most noticeable in Champaran, Patna, Monghyr and Muzaffarpur. Shahabad, however, shows an appreciable increase.

For the 3/4 Year ending 31 March 1930

Sl. No.	District	As on 1st July 1929 Schools	Pupils	1st April 1930 Schools	Pupils
1.	Patna	3	253	3	304
2.	Gaya	—	—	—	—
3.	Shahabad	2	105	2	155
4.	Saran	2	95	2	105
5.	Champaran	4	275	3	248
6.	Muzaffarpur	2	105	2	145
7.	Darbhanga	6	223	6	260
8.	Monghyr	6	257	6	257
9.	Bhagalpur	1	120	1	100
10.	Purnea	2	65	2	45
11.	Santhal Parganas	1	62	1	52
12.	Hazaribagh	—	—	—	—
13.	Ranchi	—	—	—	—
14.	Palamu	—	—	—	—
15.	Manbhum	—	—	—	—
16.	Singhbhum	1	127	1	93
	Total	30	1486	30	1542

For the Half Year ending 30 September 1930

1.	Patna	3	304	3	86
2.	Gaya	—	—	—	—
3.	Shahabad	2	155	2	95
4.	Saran	2	105	2	90
5.	Champaran	3	248	3	225
6.	Muzaffarpur	2	145	2	120
7.	Darbhanga	6	260	5	112
8.	Monghyr	6	257	6	260
9.	Bhagalpur	1	100	1	100
10.	Purnea	2	45	1	30
11.	Santhal Parganas	1	52	1	30
12.	Hazaribagh	—	—	—	—
13.	Ranchi	1	82	1	55
14.	Palamu	—	—	—	—
15.	Manbhum	—	—	—	—
16.	Singhbhum	1	93	1	37
	Total	30	1542	28	1240

Ref. : Political Special File No. 228/1930—Bihar State Archives, Patna.

Champaran shows a reducation of one school while Ranchi had added one, resulting in net loss of one school.

Although there was a noticeable decrease in the number of pupils in Champaran, Bhagalpur, Purnea, Santhal Parganas and Singhbhum had a net increase of 9%; Patna, Shahabad, Muzaffarpur and Darbhanga showing an appreciable increase, and Saran a fair increase.

For the Half Year ending 31st March 1931

Sl. No.	District	As on 1st October 1930 Schools	As on 1st October 1930 Pupils	As on 1st April 1931 Schools	As on 1st April 1931 Pupils
1.	Patna	3	86	3	202
2.	Gaya	—	—	—	—
3.	Shahabad	2	95	1	50
4.	Saran	2	90	2	99
5.	Champaran	3	225	3	156
6.	Muzaffarpur	2	120	2	105
7.	Darbhanga	5	112	5	122
8.	Monghyr	6	260	6	274
9.	Bhagalpur	1	100	1	60
10.	Purnea	1	30	1	100
11.	Santhal Parganas	1	30	1	30
12.	Hazaribagh	—	—	—	—
13.	Ranchi	1	55	1	70
14.	Palamu	—	—	—	—
15.	Manbhum	—	—	—	—
16.	Singhbhum	1	37	—	—
	Total	28	1240	26	1268

For the Half Year ending 30th September 1931

1.	Patna	3	202	3	193
2.	Gaya	—	—	—	—
3.	Shahabad	1	50	1	60
4.	Saran	2	99	1	73
5.	Champaran	3	156	2	94
6.	Muzaffarpur	2	105	2	124
7.	Darbhanga	5	122	5	173
8.	Monghyr	6	274	6	263
9.	Bhagalpur	1	60	1	60
10.	Purnea	1	100	2	148
11.	Santhal Parganas	1	30	1	53
12.	Hazaribagh	—	—	—	—
13.	Ranchi	1	70	1	80
14.	Palamu	—	—	—	—
15.	Manbhum	—	—	—	—
16.	Singhbhum	—	—	—	—
	Total	26	1268	26	1370

Ref. : Political Special File No. 231/1931—State Archives.

Shahabad and Singhbhum show a reduction of one school each, in spite of which the net decrease in pupils is only 81—approximately 6%.

For the Half Year ending 31st March 1933

Sl. No.	District	As on 1st October 1932 Schools	Pupils	As on 1st April 1933 Schools	Pupils
1.	Patna	1	74	1	65
2.	Gaya	1	40	—	—
3.	Shahabad	1	50	1	50
4.	Saran	1	40	1	57
5.	Champaran	1	71	1	90
6.	Muzaffarpur	—	—	—	—
7.	Darbhanga	3	126	3	137
8.	Monghyr	3	118	3	218
9.	Bhagalpur	—	—	—	—
10.	Purnea	—	—	—	—
11.	Santhal Parganas	—	—	—	—
12.	Hazaribagh	—	—	—	—
13.	Ranchi	1	67	1	80
14.	Palamu	—	—	—	—
15.	Manbhum	—	—	—	—
16.	Singhbhum	—	—	—	—
	Total	12	566	13	718

For the Half Year ending 30th September 1933

1.	Patna	1	65	1	60
2.	Gaya	—	—	—	—
3.	Shahabad	1	50	1	35
4.	Saran	1	57	1	51
5.	Champaran	1	90	1	93
6.	Muzaffarpur	—	—	—	—
7.	Darbhanga	3	137	3	130
8.	Monghyr	3	218	3	230
9.	Bhagalpur	—	—	—	—
10.	Purnea	1	11	1	25
11.	Santhal Parganas	1	50	1	75
12.	Hazaribagh	—	—	—	—
13.	Ranchi	1	80	1	85
14.	Palamu	—	—	—	—
15.	Manbhum	—	—	—	—
16.	Singhbhum	—	—	—	—
	Total	13	718	13	784

Ref.: Political Spl. File No. 150/1933—Bihar State Archives.

For the Half Year ending 31st March 1934

Sl. No.	District	As on 1st October 1933 Schools	Pupils	As on 1st April 1934 Schools	Pupils
1.	Patna	1	60	1	66
2.	Gaya	—	—	—	—
3.	Shahabad	1	35	1	30
4.	Saran	1	51	1	48
5.	Champaran	1	93	1	81
6.	Muzaffarpur	—	—	—	—
7.	Darbhanga	3	130	3	132
8.	Monghyr	3	230	2	205
9.	Bhagalpur	—	—	—	—
10.	Purnea	1	25	2	28
11.	Santhal Parganas	1	75	1	96
12.	Hazaribagh	—	—	—	—
13.	Ranchi	1	85	1	104
14.	Palamu	—	—	—	—
15.	Manbhum	—	—	—	—
16.	Singhbhum	—	—	—	—
	Total	13	784	13	790

For the Half Year ending 30th September 1934

1.	Patna	1	66	1	53
2.	Gaya	—	—	—	—
3.	Shahabad	1	30	1	32
4.	Saran	1	48	1	36
5.	Champaran	1	81	1	83
6.	Muzaffarpur	—	—	—	—
7.	Darbhanga	3	132	3	142
8.	Monghyr	2	205	2	220
9.	Bhagalpur	—	—	—	—
10.	Purnea	2	28	2	46
11.	Santhal Parganas	1	96	1	90
12.	Hazaribagh	—	—	—	—
13.	Ranchi	1	104	1	101
14.	Palamu	—	—	—	—
15.	Manbhum	—	—	—	—
16.	Singhbhum	—	—	—	—
	Total	13	790	13	803

Ref.: Political Spl. File No. 114/1934—Bihar State Archives.

For the Half Year ending 31st March 1935

Sl. No.	District	As on 1st October 1934 Schools	Pupils	As on 1st April 1935 Schools	Pupils
1.	Patna	1	53	1	49
2.	Gaya	—	—	—	—
3.	Shahabad	1	32	1	50
4.	Saran	1	36	1	45
5.	Champaran	1	83	1	72
6.	Muzaffarpur	—	—	—	—
7.	Darbhanga	3	142	6	292
8.	Monghyr	2	220	5	328
9.	Bhagalpur	—	—	—	—
10.	Purnea	2	46	2	45
11.	Santhal Parganas	1	90	1	99
12.	Hazaribagh	—	—	—	—
13.	Ranchi	1	101	1	102
14.	Palamu	—	—	—	—
15.	Manbhum	—	—	—	—
16.	Singhbhum	—	—	—	—
	Total	13	803	19	882

For the Half Year ending 30th September 1935

1.	Patna	1	49	1	71
2.	Gaya	—	—	—	—
3.	Shahabad	1	50	1	30
4.	Saran	1	45	1	40
5.	Champaran	1	72	1	63
6.	Muzaffarpur	—	—	—	—
7.	Dharbhanga	6	292	6	292
8.	Monghyr	5	328	5	328
9.	Bhagalpur	—	—	—	—
10.	Purnea	2	45	2	45
11.	Santhal Parganas	1	99	1	99
12.	Hazaribagh	—	—	—	—
13.	Ranchi	1	102	1	102
14.	Palamu	—	—	—	—
15.	Manbhum	—	—	—	—
16.	Singbhum	—	—	—	—
	Total	19	1082	19	1070

Ref.: Political Spl. File No. 168/1935.

APPENDIX II

List of Purses and Contributions received by Gandhiji during his 'Harijan Tour' in Bihar, during the year 1934, for the Upliftment of Harijans (*Harijan*, 8 June 1934)

Date	*Rs.*	*Annas*	*Paise*	*Patna*
1	*2*	*3*	*4*	*5*
13-3-'34	20	0	0	By a lady
	20	0	0	By a friend
	1	0	0	—do—
				Champaran District
15 to 17 March	210	3	0	Collection made by Gandhiji during his tour in the Dist.
	6	0	0	—do—
	10	0	0	—do—
	11	4	0	—do—
18, 19 March	10	0	0	Miscellaneous—Patna By S.M. Desai, by cheque
				Patna
20 March	8	0	0	By Sarjubala
	8	0	0	Misc.
	5	0	0	in public meeting, Patna

1	2	3	4	5
22 to 24	8	0	0	Misc. at Autograph
March	100	0	0	Misc. collection from Hemlata Devi of Dewas
25, 26	250	8	0	Purse by public
March	122	6	6	Misc. collection
	20	0	0	Autograph and Misc.
				Patna District
17, 28 March	91	0	0	Sale proceeds of ornaments, Patna
29, 30, 31 March	10	0	0	Misc. from Ramlal Chaudhary of Hajipur
				Patna
1 to 5 April	7	0	0	Miscellaneous
				Dinapur, Patna Dist.
	200	0	0	Miscellaneous

Collection made by Gandhiji in Tour in Different Parts of Bihar

27 March	5	0	0	Prasadi (Saran Dist.)
	12	0	0	Kahara (Saran Dist.)
	25	0	0	Masarakh (Saran Dist.)
	15	0	0	Miscellaneous
20 March	276	4	11	Miscellaneous
	30	0	0	Misc.
	27	2	3	Sonepur Station
	55	2	0	Hajipur (Muzaffarpur Dist.)
	85	4	5	Muzaffarpur
	10	1	7	Miscellaneous
	50	8	0	Dighwara (Saran Dist.)

1	*2*	*3*	*4*	*5*
29 March	24	14	10½	Belsand (Muzaffarpur Dist.)
	25	8	0	Chandauli —do—
	5	8	0	Moch —do—
	5	8	0	Tunigach —do—
	75	5	9	Sitamarhi —do—
30 March	27	0	0	Sitamarhi —do—
	4	0	0	Darbhanga (Darbhanga Dist.)
	60	13	0	Kamtaul —do—
	70	9	8	Darbhanga —do—
	129	9	10½	Pupari —do—
1 April	25	8	0	Naraiya —do—
	76	8	0	Nirmali (Bhagalpur Dist.)
	3	0	0	Supaul —do—
	77	2	11½	Sukhapur —do—
2 April	15	0	11½	Saharsa —do—
	1	8	0	Saharsa —do—
	52	3	5	Bihapur —do—
	13	5	5	Babhangaon —do—
	500	0	0	Bhagalpur —do—
	347	4	10	Bhagalpur —do—
	43	3	11½	Sultanganj —do—
	25	8	0	Banka Local Board, Bhag.
	25	8	0	Navabgadh (Monghyr Dist.)
	113	4	9	Monghyr

1	*2*	*3*	*4*	*5*
4 April	66	3	3	Jamalpur (Monghyr Dist.)
	172	11	11½	Budhaiya —do—
	85	15	0	Sianar (Patna District)
	73	5	11½	Pandarak —do—
	34	9	3	Mukama —do—
	112	8	0	Bakhtiarpur —do—
	322	3	3	Mukama Thana —do—
	124	13	3	Barhgama —do—
	50	0	0	Miscellaneous —do—
	13	8	3	Matida —do—
5 April	32	0	0	*Muzaffarpur District*, price of ornaments
	34	0	0	*Patna District*, price of ornaments
	32	0	0	Bhagalpur Dist., price of ornaments
	32	0	0	Darbhanga Dist., —do—
	22	0	0	Patna
	3	0	0	Hajipur
	4	0	0	Motihari (Champaran)
6 April	250	0	0	By Shri Prabhuchan Gayawala
	12	0	0	Misc., Patna
	123	0	0	Dinapur (Patna Dist.)
	17	0	0	Misc., Bhagalpur Dist.

1	*2*	*3*	*4*	*5*
8 April	12	6	3	Misc., collection from Sonepur to Nawgachia
	43	0	0	Purse by Nawgachia people
	5	3	0	Collection at Nawagachia Station, Purnea
	3	4	3	Demapur station collection
	54	5	5	Katihar ,, ,,
	5	6	8	,, ,, ,,
	3	10	6	Routed ,, ,,
	2	10	6	Purnea ,, ,,
	3	8	6	Kasaba ,, ,,
	12	8	0	Gurupalia students
	1	3	0	Misc. at Gurupalia station
	47	5	9	Collection at Forbesganj & Phulkah, Purnea Dist.
9 April	22	14	0	Collection at residence for Arreriya
	15	10	3	—do— Kasba station, Purnea
	25	8	0	By Manuman Bux
	125	0	0	Addresses of Purnea Municipality auctioned to Mrs. Bir Narayan
	127	11	6	Misc. collection, Purnea Dist.
10 April	134	9	6	Tikkapath Ashram, Karhagola and Semapurist
	20	0	0	Kasaba, by citizens of Katihar

1	2	3	4	5
				Purnea District
	9	15	0	Collection at Sonnailly station
	13	13	3	—do— Barsoi station
	50	0	0	Shri Mrityunjaya Prasad
	11	9	3	Collection at Barauni station
	6	2	9	Railway station collection
	5	2	9	Sonnailly station ,,
	5	5	6	Misc. collection, Purnea
	125	0	0	Payment by Chaudhary P.C. Lal
				Katihar
	6	15	6	By rice and oil mills
	19	0	6	Misc. collection at station
	7	0	0	Collection at Semapur ,,
	4	9	9	Collection at Kadhagola ,,
	9	1	3	Collection at Nawgachia ,,
				Thana Bihpur
	24	8	8	Station collection
	55	6	8	Mansiry station
	30	15	9	Khagadia ,,
				Monghyr District
	11	1	6	Barauni Jn. station
	23	8	1	Parani ,, ,,
	8	12	6	Bachhwara ,,
	7	7	9	Tilsing Sarai ,,

1	*2*	*3*	*4*	*5*
				Darbhanga District
	257	0	0	Samastipur purse
	46	5	10	„ station collection
				Muzaffarpur District
	159	13	6	Open collection in meeting at Gokhlepur (Muzaffarpur)
24 April	89	0	0	Dhamaur village purse
	33	5	0	Muzaffarpur station and from Khaddar auctions
	19	5	0	Bhusura village collection
	13	15	9	Goraul „ „
	8	3	9	Bhagwanpur „ „
	17	3	2	Misc. collection at Sonepur and other stations
25 April				*Patna*
	6	10	0	Misc. collection
	5	0	0	Dasrath Lal, Bihta
				Arrah District
	13	1	6	Koilwar station collection
	165	0	0	Purse and Misc. collection from Jamirapur Radha Mohan Sinha
				Arrah
	490	1	0	Purse by citizens
	500	0	0	Purse by Raja Saheb of Surajpur
	51	0	0	By Sangit Samaj of Arrah

1	2	3	4	5
	180	4	6	Misc. at residence
	5	1	0	Misc. collection at station
	5	0	0	Purse by Dhanadia village
	6	6	6	Collection at station
	41	0	0	Purse by Bihia village
	101	0	0	Purse by Musammat Dharikshana
	29	0	0	Purse by anonymous friend
	21	0	0	Anonymous
	31	8	8	Anonymous
	231	3	0	Purse by Mahajana
	38	8	0	Misc. collection at Burhanpur Thana
	51	0	0	Purse by Rajpur Thana
	175	9	6	Misc. collection in Buxar meeting
	7	2	6	Dumraon station collection
	20	8	4	Arrah station collection
	20	5	8	Misc. „ „
	165	0	0	„ „ „
				Deoghar
	10	0	0	Purse by Suniti Devi
	600	0	0	Purse by citizens
	328	7	11	Misc. collection
	51	0	0	By Ganesh Prasad Sah
	11	0	0	Anonymous
	172	0	0	Misc. collection
	85	0	0	„ „

1	2	3	4	5
				Monghyr District
	43	7	6	Collection at Rly. Station
	5	0	0	Purse by Hindu Mahasabha of Sethpur
	24	6	6	Misc. collection (Sethpur)
	105	1	0	Purse by Nawada people
	33	3	0	Purse by Marsaligan people
27 April	251	0	0	Raja Saheb of Tekari
	160	0	0	Collection in ladies' meeting
	117	5	6	Purse from Tekari people
	365	0	0	Purse by citizens of Gaya
	4	0	6	Purse by Vidyapith Mandal of Gaya
	550	0	0	Misc. collection at autograph
	240	9	6	Misc. collection
	50	0	0	Autograph to Sidheshwar Singh
	129	3	1	Misc. collection at ladies' meeting
				Sherghati
	101	0	0	Purse at Sherghati
				Chhapra
	50	2	3	Purse by citizens
	177	15	3	Misc. collection in meeting
	1	8	3	Misc. collection in meeting

1	2	3	4	5
				Hazaribagh
	50	0	0	Misc. collection at residence
	35	0	0	Ladies' purse
	94	1	8	,, meeting collection
	497	0	6	Purse by citizens
	40	0	0	Misc. collection
	7	0	0	,, ,,
	88	10	4	,, ,,
28 April	20	0	0	,, ,,
	24	0	0	,, ,,
	31	9	3	,, ,,
	17	6	6	Purse by Bishnugarh people
	85	11	9	,, ,, Gomio people
				Bermo (Dist. Hazaribagh)
	2152	0	0	Purse by citizens
	33	3	0	,, ,, coolies
	27	3	3	,, ,, Dumari Anchal
	210	7	9	,, ,, Ladies
	251	0	0	,, ,, Madhovjee
				Katrasgarh (Dist. Haz.)
	301	0	0	Citizens' purse
	19	0	0	Misc. auction
	48	12	0	Misc. collection
				Jharia (Manbhum Dist.)
	178	1	0	Purse by citizens
	45	0	0	Misc. collection
	7	0	0	,, ,,
	1052	0	0	Purse by citizens
	193	1	9	Misc. collection

1	*2*	*3*	*4*	*5*
29 April				*Jharia*
	10	0	0	Autograph
				Jamdoba
	701	0	0	Tata Colliery Workers' purse
	135	0	0	Misc. auction
	55	0	0	Misc. collection
	44	14	2	Misc. collection at public meeting

Bibliography

Books

Andrews, C.F., *The Renaissance in India*, Bombay, 1956.

Azad, A.K., *India Wins Freedom*, Bombay, 1959.

Abdullah, Yusuf Ali, *A Cultural History of India during the British Period*, Bombay, 1940.

Ahmad, Aziz, *Studies in Islamic Culture in the Indian Environment*, Oxford, 1964.

Bhatia, B.M., *History and Social Development*, Vols. I & II, Vikas Publishing House, New Delhi, 1974, 1977.

Buchanan, *A Journey from Madras*, Vol. I, 1813.

Bhai, Narendra, *Lok Kranti Pathey*, Ed., Varanasi, 1981.

Banes, *Cotton Manufacture in India.*

Bamford, P.C., *Histories of the Non-Cooperation and Khilafat Movements*, printed by Government of India, 1925.

Banerjee, S.N., *A Nation in Making*, Calcutta, 1964.

Bhagwan, Vishnu, *Constitutional History of India and National Movement*, 1972.

Bal Krishna, *Commercial Relations between India and England*, London, 1924.

Barns, Margarita, 1. *India, Today & Tomorrow*, 1937.
2. *The Indian Press*, 1940.

Chambers, *20th Century Dictionary.*

Chirol, Valentine, *Indian Unrest*, London, 1910.

Chopra, P.N., *Who is Who of Indian Martyrs*, Vol. I, Government of India Publication, New Delhi, 1969.

Chandra, Bipin, *The Rise and Growth of Economic Nationalism in India*, Delhi, 1966.

Das, M.N., *History of Freedom Movement*, 2 volumes.

Dodwell, Henry, *A New History of India*, Allahabad, 1965.

Diwakar, R.R., *Bihar through the Ages*, Orient Longmans, Bombay, Calcutta, Madras, New Delhi, 1959.

Datta, K.K., *History of the Freedom Movement in Bihar*, Vols. I & II, 1947 & 1957.

Datta, K.K., *The Writings and Speeches of Mahatma Gandhi*, Published by Govt. of Bihar, Patna, 1960.

Datta, K.K., *The Comprehensive History of Bihar* (Ed.), Vol. III, Parts I, II, Patna, 1976.

Datta, K.K., *India's March to Freedom*, 1949.

Datta, Bhupendra N., *Dvitiya Swadhintar Sangram*, Calcutta, 1949.

Desai, Mahadev, *Gandhiji in Indian Villages*, Delhi, 1959.

———, *Encyclopaedia of Social Science*, Vols. IX-X.

Desai, A.R., *Social Background to Indian Nationalism*, Bombay, 1959.

Digby, William, '*Prosperous*' *British India*, London, 1901.

Dutt, R.P., *India Today* (*1949*).

Fairchild, H.P., *Dictionary of Sociology*.

Fisher, Louis, *The Life of Mahatma Gandhi*, New York, 1950.

Fredrick, John Shore, *Notes on India Affairs*, Vol. I, 1937.

Gadgil, D.R., *Industrial Evolution in India in Recent Times*, 1860-1939, OUP, 1971.

Ganguli, B.N., *Gandhi's Social Philosophy*, Delhi, 1973.

Geoffrey, Ashe, *Gandhi, A Study in Revolution*, Bombay, 1968.

Ghosh, D.R., *The Industrial Guide*.

Hoebel, E.A., *Man in the Primitive World*.

Holwell, *India Tracts*.

Hamid, Abdul, *Muslim Separatism in India*, OUP, Lahore, 1976.

Houlton, Sir J., *Bihar, The Heart of India.*

Heimsath, Charles H., *Indian Nationalism and Hindu Social Reform*, Princeton, 1964.

Haque, Mazharul, *The Great Trial of Mahatma Gandhi.*

James Mill, *History of India*, Vol. III.

Kripalani, J.B., *Gandhi's Life and Thoughts.*

Lal Bahadur, *The Muslim League, its Activities and Achievements*, Agra, 1954.

Lewis, Arthur W., *Economic Survey*, 1919-1939, London, 1949.

Marx & Engels, *Collected Works*, Moscow, 1950.

Marx, Karl, *A Contribution to the Critique of Political Economy*, Moscow, 1970.

Majumdar, B.B. & Majumdar, B.P., *Congress and Congressmen*, Calcutta, 1967.

Mahatma Gandhi, *Autobiography*, Ahmedabad, 1956.

Mahatma Gandhi, *The Constructive Programmes*, Navjivan Prakashan, Ahmedabad.

Mahatma Gandhi, *Young India* (1919-21), Madras, 1922 (1922-24) and (1924-26), Madras, 1927 (1927-28).

Majumdar, R.C., *History of the Freedom Movement in India*, Vols. I, II, III.

Majumdar, R.C., *History and Culture of Indian People*, Vols. X, XI, Bombay, 1963.

Malviya, H.D., *Socialist Ideology of Congress*, Delhi, 1966.

Mehrotra, S.R., *The Emergence of Indian National Congress*, Delhi, 1971.

Mehta & Patwardhan, *The Communal Triangle*, Allahabad, 1954.

Mitra, Shishir Kr., *Sri Aurobindo and Indian Freedom.*

Mishra, B.B., *Mahatma Gandhi's Movement in Champaran*, 1960.

Mishra, B.B, *The Central Administration of the East India Company*, 1959.

Mookherji, D.P., *Modern Indian Culture*, Bombay, 1948.

Moon, P., *Divide and Quit*, London, 1962.

Nehru, Jawahar Lal, *Discovery of India*, London, 1956.

Narayan, Baldeo, *August Kranti.*

O'Mally, L.S.S., *History of Bengal, Bihar and Orissa under British Rule*, Calcutta, 1925.

Page, C.H., *Class, Status, Power.*

Pandey, B.N., *Rise of Modern India*, London, 1967.

Panikkar, K.M., *Asian and Western Dominance*, London, 1953.

Prasad, Bisheshwar, *Bondage & Freedom.*

Prasad, Ishwari, *A New History of India*, Allahabad, 1965.

Prasad, Rajendra, *Atmakatha*, Ahmedabad, 1948.

Prasad, Rajendra, *Mahatma Gandhi and Bihar*, Delhi, 1957.

Prasad, Rajendra, *Gandhi in Champaran*, Delhi, 1955.

Prasad, Rajendra, *Satyagraha in Champaran*, Delhi, 1955.

Prasad, Rajendra, *Autobiography*, Bombay, 1957.

Prasad, Rajendra, *Champaran Men Mahatma Gandhi*, Delhi, 1955.

Prasad, Rajendra, *The Constructive Programmes of Mahatma Gandhi—Some Suggestions.*

Prasad, Rajendra, *Bapu Ke Kadmon Men* (Hindi), 1950.

Prasad, Rajendra, *India Divided.*

Prasad, Janakdhari, *Kuchh Apni Kuchh Desh Ki*, Muzaffarpur, 1970.

Prasad, Janakdhari, *Autobiography*, Part I.

Pal, Bipin Chandra, *Swadeshi and Swaraj*, Calcutta, 1954.

Prizada, Syed Sharfuddin, *Foundation of Pakistan*, 1906-47, Karachi, 1970, two volumes (Ed.).

Rudolph & Rudolph, *The Modernity of Tradition*, Bombay, 1967.

Revolution & Revolution, Collection of Karl Marx's articles, published in New York, *Tribune*, 1851-52.

Roy, Lala Lajpat, *History of the Arya Samaj*, 1914.

Roychaudhury, P.C., *Insider Bihar*, 1962.

Roychaudhury, P.C., *B.R.D.G. Champaran* (Ed.).

Singh, Baljit, *Urban Middle Class Climber*.

Singh, D. & Ramgopal, *Indian Politics from Crown Rule to Independence*, Aligadh, 1968.

Singh, H., *Early European Banking in India*, 1927.

Singh, Anugrah Narayan, *Mere Sansmaran* (Hindi).

Singh, Sitaram, *Nationalism and Social Reform in India*, (1885-1920), Delhi, 1968.

Seal, Anil, *The Emergence of Indian Nationalism*, Cambridge, 1968.

Shastri, Chandra Shekhar, *Bharatiye Atankwad ka Itihas* (Hindi).

Sharma, S.R., *The Making of Modern India*, Bombay, 1951.

Sinha, Sachchidanand, *Some Eminent Bihar Contemporaries*, 1944.

Singh, Anugrah Narayan, *Abhinandan Granth*.

Singh, Arjun Pd., *Bihpur Satyagraha*, 1930.

Shrikrishna, *Abhinandan Granth*.

Sitaramayya, B. Pattabhi, *History of the Indian National Congress*, Vols. I & II.

Srinivas, M.N., *Social Change in Modern India*.

Tara Chand, *History of the Freedom Movement in India*, Vols. I, II, III, Ministry of Information & Communication, 1967, 1972.

Trevelyan, C.E., *On the Education of People of India*, London, 1838.

———, *The Civil Disobedience Movement*, Govt. of India Press, New Delhi, 1956.

Tendulkar, D.G., *Mahatma*, Vols. III, IV, 1-8, Bombay, 1951-54.

Vachaspati, Indra Vidya, *Arya Samaj ka Itihas*, Vol. II.

Verma, Kamla Pd., *Bhulti Bhagti Yaden* (Hindi).

Watt, George, *Economic Products of India*, seven volumes, Delhi, 1889.

———, *Sampurna Gandhi Bangmaya* (Hindi), Vols. 16 to 70, Information & Broadcasting Ministry, Govt. of India, 1979.

Journals & Newspapers

The Biharee, Patna.

The Bihar Herald, Patna.

The Balak.

The Bihar Darpan, Muzaffarpur.

The Bihar Times.

The Kayastha Samachar.

The Calcutta Review.

The Express, Allahabad.

Friend of India.

The Searchlight, Patna.

The Patliputra.

The Indian Nation, Patna.

The Tribune.

The Times of India.

The Young India, Ahmedabad.

The Yugantar.

The Hindustan Review.

The Modern Review.

Journal of Bihar & Orissa Research.

Man in India.

Harijan, from 1920 to 1939.

Reports & Returns and other Government Publications

Bihar, Year to Year : Bihar Government Administration Report.

Bihar & Orissa, Year to Year.

Bulletins of the Indian National Congress.

Presidential Address of the Indian National Congress from 1920 (Annual).

Proceedings and Reports of the Indian National Congress from 1920.

Proceedings and Reports of Indian Social Conference (Annual, 10th, 1887).

Proceedings of the Bihar and Orissa Legislative Council.

All Parties' Conference, 1928 : Report (Supplementary) of the Committee.

Report of the Civil Disobedience Enquiry Committee, 1922.

Indian Statistical Abstract (Annual).

The Moral and Material Progress : Reports.

The Indian Annual Register.

Bihar District Gazetteers.

Imperial Gazetteers of India.

Bengal Directory (Commercial), 1835.

Sketch of Commercial Resources.

Reports on the Census of India, Vol. V, Bengal, Bihar, Orissa, Sikkim, 1913.

Bihar Regional Records Committee's Report.

Quinquennial Review on the Progress of Education in Bihar & Orissa.

Proceedings of Imperial Legislative Council.

First Decennial Review (1912-22) : Bihar & Orissa.

The Indian Year Book.

The Annual India Quarterly Register.

All India Congress Committee's Annual Report.

Bihar Provincial Congress Committee's Report.

Annual Report of the Congress Secretaries.

Weekly Report of the Provincial Congress Committee.

Bihar Political Conference Report.

Reports on Political Events in Bihar, Fortnightly Report, Bihar.

Bihar Police Administration Report.

Reports of the Superintendents of Police.

Police Reports.

Fortnightly Reports of Patna Commissioner.

Reports of the Secretaries of Provincial Anti-Untouchability League.

Reports of the Secretaries, Provincial Khaddar Board.

The Non-Cooperation & Khilafat Movements in Bihar & Orissa, etc.

Reports of the Bihar Vidyapith and its affiliated Institutions, Patna.

Bihar Gazette, Extra-ordinary, August 1942.

Proceeding Book of Bihar Provincial Congress Committee, Sadaquat Ashram, Patna.

Census Reports for 1921, 1931 & 1941.

Unpublished Records

Unpublished Records of National Archives, New Delhi.
Unpublished Records of Bengal, Calcutta.
Unpublished Records of State Archives, Bihar, Patna.
Unpublished Records of Divisional and District Offices of Bihar.
These include—
Proceedings,
Consultations,
Reports,
Diaries
and correspondence of various officers
contained in Confidential Files of Bihar
Political (Special) Department,
Home Political Department Files;
and Bihar & Orissa Police Abstract of Intelligence.

Index